走向世界

国际理解教育实践研究

冯晓颖 著

哈尔滨工程大学出版社
Harbin Engineering University Press

U0645437

内 容 简 介

　　本书以英语课标为依据、以课程建设为引导、以科研课题为引领、以优秀课例为示范，突破英语教学难点，整合英语阅读素材。全书分为四章，分别为魅力中学、魅力世界、国际公民、大湾区变化，旨在用英语讲好中国故事，用英语讲出文化自信。本书在培养学生具有国际视野、增强包容意识、尊重文化差异、树立共同发展理念等方面，具有一定的实践价值。

　　本书可供初中生及英语阅读爱好者阅读及使用。

图书在版编目(CIP)数据

　　走向世界：国际理解教育实践研究/冯晓颖著. —
哈尔滨:哈尔滨工程大学出版社，2023.6
　　ISBN 978-7-5661-3931-3

　　Ⅰ.①走… Ⅱ.①冯… Ⅲ.①国情教育-教学研究-
中小学 Ⅳ.①G633.202

　　中国国家版本馆 CIP 数据核字(2023)第 091451 号

走向世界——国际理解教育实践研究
ZOUXIANG SHIJIE—GUOJI LIJIE JIAOYU SHIJIAN YANJIU

选题策划　王丽华
责任编辑　王丽华
封面设计　李海波

出版发行	哈尔滨工程大学出版社
社　　址	哈尔滨市南岗区南通大街 145 号
邮政编码	150001
发行电话	0451-82519328
传　　真	0451-82519699
经　　销	新华书店
印　　刷	黑龙江天宇印务有限公司
开　　本	787 mm×1 092 mm　1/16
印　　张	8
字　　数	155 千字
版　　次	2023 年 6 月第 1 版
印　　次	2023 年 6 月第 1 次印刷
定　　价	48.00 元

http://www.hrbeupress.com
E-mail:heupress@ hrbeu.edu.cn

目　　录
Contents

第一章 魅力中学
Chapter 1 Charming Middle School

初中是人生的黄金时期,这个时期是人体生长发育的最佳时期,也是人生的第一个转折的关键时期。九月初,青少年沐浴着秋日金色的阳光,迈进了初中的大门,开启了中学的学习生活。新的学校、新的班级、新的同学、新的老师,似乎一切都那么新鲜,那么有趣。在中学,你可以学习丰富的课程,参加多彩的社团活动和各项研学活动,接受生命教育,每一件事物都有它的独到之处,都有神秘之感,每一项体验都充满魅力。初中的生活绚烂无比,像灿烂的图画。

The period of junior middle school is the golden years of human life. This period is not only the best period for human body growth and gradual psychological maturity, but also the first turning point in life. In early September, young people bask in the autumn golden sun, enter into the door of junior middle school and start the middle school learning. The new school, the new class, the new classmates, the new teachers all seem so fresh and interesting. In middle school, you can learn rich courses, participate in varied clubs and the activities of research and study, accept life education. Everything has its own uniqueness and mystery. Every experience is full of charm. Junior middle school life is gorgeous, like brilliant pictures.

第一节 丰富课程
Section 1 Rich Courses

身边小事 Little Things around Us

　　九月,金金和湾湾迎来了新的学期。他们成为初一年级的学生了。瞧! 同学们正在操场上参加开学典礼。初中是他们人生的一个新阶段。它意味着他们将背负更多的责任。在中学里,他们不仅可以在知识的海洋中遨游,还能体验不同的校园活动,结交更多的朋友。

　　In September, JinJin and Wanwan are having a new term. They become middle school students of Grade One. Look! The students are taking part in the opening ceremony on the playground. Junior high school is a new stage of their life. It means they will have more responsibilities. In middle school, they can not only enjoy the ocean of knowledge, but also experience different campus activities and make more friends.

大家共言 Common Topic

　　进入初中后,学生们有着丰富且有趣的课程。一起来瞧瞧吧!

　　After entering junior high school, students have rich and interesting courses. Let's have a look!

　　语文课可以帮助学生提高语言文字的表达能力。学生们可以通过学习语文来培养自己的爱国情怀。学习语文是很有必要的。学生们只有认真地学习语文,才能更好地阅读一些名家作品。

　　Chinese lesson can help students improve their language expression ability. Students can cultivate their patriotic feelings through learning Chinese. It is necessary to learn Chinese. Only when students study Chinese carefully can they read some famous works better.

语文课　**Chinese Lesson**

数学是帮助人类认识世界的一门科学,值得每个人去学习。数学可以锻炼人的思维能力,如计算能力、逻辑思维能力。随着社会的发展,科技变得越来越发达。每个人都应该掌握一定的数学知识来提高自己的社会竞争力。

Math is a science for human beings to understand the world. It is worth learning for everyone. Math can train people's thinking ability, such as calculating ability and logical thinking ability. With the development of society, technology is becoming more and more developed. Everyone should master a certain amount of mathematical knowledge to improve their social competitiveness.

数学课　**Math Lesson**

英语作为世界通用语言,是联合国的工作语言之一。随着全球化的到来,英语的使用变得更加广泛。掌握一定的英语技能可以帮助我们结交外国的朋友,体验不同的文化。

As the world's common language, English is one of the working languages of the United Nations. With the arrival of globalization, English has been used more and more widely. Mastering certain English skills can help us make foreign friends and experience different cultures.

英语课　English Lesson

随着互联网的快速发展,越来越多的学校开设了计算机课程。现在是互联网时代,因此,我们每个人都需要学习一些计算机技能。这些技能不仅能使我们的学习变得更加简单,还能让我们认识到更广阔的世界!

With the rapid development of Internet, more and more schools offer computer courses. It is the Internet era, so, each of us need to learn some computer skills. These skills not only make our learning easier, but also enable us to recognize a wider world!

计算机课　Computer Lesson

化学是人类用以认识和改造物质世界的主要方法之一,它与人类进步和社会发展的关系非常密切。

Chemistry is one of the main methods used by human beings to understand and transform the material world. It is closely related to human progress and social development.

化学课　**Chemistry Lesson**

除了上面介绍的课程外,还有很多课程,如体育课、生物课、物理课和音乐课等。

In addition to the courses described above, there are many courses such as P. E. lesson, biology lesson, physics lesson and music lesson and so on.

体育课　**P. E. Lesson**

生物课　**Biology Lesson**

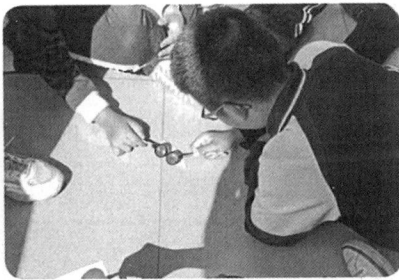

物理课 **Physics Lesson**

音乐课 **Music Lesson**

你认为中国初中生的校园生活精彩吗?

Do you think the campus life of junior high school students in China is wonderful?

少年观天下 Youth's View of the World

让我们来看看美国的初中生都有哪些课程吧!他们也学习物理、数学、化学等。除此之外,美国人似乎更注重对学生动手能力的培养,因此他们还开设一些厨艺课。厨艺课使学生可以感受到妈妈的辛苦并且培养了他们的学习能力。

Let's take a look at the courses offered by junior high school students in the United States. They also study physics, math, chemistry and so on. Besides, Americans seem to pay more attention to the cultivation of students' practical ability, so they also offer some cooking lessons. The cooking lessons enable students to feel their mothers' hard work and develop their learning ability.

厨艺课　**Cooking Lesson**

　　在英国又是怎样的呢？除了学习类似于我们语文课的英国文学,他们还要学习西班牙语、法语、德语。还有同学选修了汉语。当然还有许多有趣的课程,比如戏剧、烹饪等。他们都是在玩中学习这些课程,学起来既开心又有收获。

　　What is it like in Britain? Besides English literature like our Chinese lesson, they have to learn Spanish, French and German. And then some classmates choose Chinese. Of course, there are many interesting courses, such as drama, cooking and so on. They are all learning these courses while playing. Learning them is fun and rewarding.

戏剧课　**Drama Lesson**

　　法国初中的课程安排和设置与我国没有太大的差异。只是学生的选择多一些,有两门课程——技术课和国民教育是我们国内没有的。技术课主要教学生制作东西,国民教育则教导学生了解公民意识和公民权利。

　　There is not much difference between French junior middle school curriculum arrangement and our country. Students only have more choices. Technology lesson and civic education are not available in our country. Technology lesson mainly teach students to make things, and civic education is to teach students to understand civic awareness and civil rights.

技术课 **Technology Lesson**

国民教育 **Civic Education**

澳大利亚的课程设置非常多样化,除了常规的英语、数学、物理、化学、生物、音乐、戏剧、舞蹈等,还有很多其他课程,诸如第二外语。大部分学校会把汉语、法语、日语等列为第二外语。

Australian course is very diverse. Besides regular English, math, physics, chemistry, biology, music, drama, dance and so on, there are many other courses, such as the second foreign language. Most schools use Chinese, French, Japanese etc. as a second foreign language.

除此之外,大部分的学校还会开设工艺课程,例如木制工艺、金属工艺、厨艺、农艺等。对学生身体素质以及领导素质培养的户外教育、学生领导力等课程也越来越多地出现在很多学校。

In addition, most schools also offer craft courses, such as wood crafts, metal crafts, cooking, agronomy and so on. For the outdoor education of students' physical quality and leadership quality training, students' leadership and other courses are appearing more and more frequently in many schools.

工艺课 **Craft Lesson**

活动体验馆　Activity Experience Pavilion

　　你能和同学谈论一些中国课程与国外课程的相同点和不同点吗？请说出你的感受。你更喜欢哪个国家的课程？你最喜欢什么科目？为什么？请把它们写下来。

　　Can you talk with your classmates about the similarities and differences between Chinese courses and foreign courses? Please tell me how you feel. Which country's courses do you prefer? What's your favorite subject? Why? Please write them down.

国家 Country	相同点 Similarities	不同点 Differences	最喜欢的科目 Favorite subject	为什么 Why
美国 America				
英国 Britain				
法国 France				
澳大利亚 Australia				
其他国家 Other countries				

第二节 多彩社团
Section 2　Rich and Varied Clubs

身边小事 Little Things around Us

　　湾湾是珠海的一名交换生,她要去英国学习一年。为了更好地了解国外的校园文化,更快地融入英国本土的学习生活,她想要了解更多的校园社团活动。

　　Wanwan is an exchange student in Zhuhai, she is going to study in Britain for one year. In order to understand the campus culture and integrate the study life of Britain, she wants to know more about campus club activities.

大家共言 Common Topic

　　社团文化代表学校的特色,社团文化是丰富多彩的。社团在学校扮演着重要的角色,能促进学生的身心健康。你知道多彩的社团还有多个不同的英文称谓吗?

　　The club culture represents the school's characteristic, which is rich and colorful. Club plays a very important role in school because they promote students' well-being. Do you know that colorful clubs have many different English titles?

♥国际象棋社团 Chess Club

国际象棋是世界上流行了几个世纪的一项有趣的游戏。它是一种经过国际认证的学术学习工具,适合所有年龄段的学生,以此提高他们的逻辑推理和解决问题的能力。国际象棋让学生在竞争环境中发展记忆力和专注力、战术和战略思维、自律和体育精神。国际象棋社团通常提供非正式的比赛和锦标赛,有时也提供联赛。

Chess is a fascinating game played for centuries throughout the world. It is a proven, internationally recognized academic learning tool that suits students of all ages to improve their logical reasoning and problem-solving skills. Chess develops memory and concentration, tactical and strategic thinking, self-discipline and sportsmanship in a competitive environment. Chess clubs often provide for both informal games and tournaments and sometimes offer leagues.

♥艺术社团 Art Club

艺术社团是一个学生聚集和让他们的创造力可以流动的地方。在这里,学生热爱艺术,欣赏艺术家的作品,创作自己的作品。艺术社团的使命是激发、培养和促进学生对艺术的兴趣,培养学生的美术素养。

Art club is a place where students gather and let their creativity flow. In the club, students are passionate about art, they admire artists' works and create their own works. The mission of art club is to stimulate, foster and promote students' interest in the arts and cultivate the students' artistic literacy.

♥科学社团 Science Club

科学社团是通过互动和创新的实践科学活动、项目、实验和科学事务来促进学校科研文化的组织。该社团的宗旨是弘扬科技,激发学生的积极性。

Science club is an organization that promotes scientific research culture in school through interactive and innovative hands-on science activities, projects, experiments and science affairs. The purpose of this club is to promote science and technology, and stimulate students' enthusiasm.

♥义工社团 Volunteering Club

美国社会非常看重人的奉献和服务精神。据调查,半数美国人平均每年做义工的时间大约为 100 个小时,这相当于在美国 1.5 亿成人中,每人每 3~4 天就会做 1 小时的义工服务。在这样的社会环境中成长的美国小孩子自然而然地形成了这样的认知。

American society values people's dedication and service very much. According to the survey, half of Americans spend about 100 hours a year doing volunteer work, which is equivalent to one hour of volunteer work every 3 to 4 days for 150 million adults in the United States. Growing up in such a social environment, American students naturally form this perception.

♥读书会 Book Club

学生热爱阅读,讨论书籍、作者和写作背后的创意。他们主持书籍讨论,回应书籍论坛中的帖子、辩论主题与作者。

Students love reading and discussing books, authors and the big ideas behind the writing. They lead book discussions, respond to posts in the book forum and debate topics and authors.

♥环境保护社团 Environmental Protection Club

学生关心空气和水的清洁,保护野生动物,使我们的星球对我们以及子孙后代都是安全的.

Students care about keeping air and water clean, our wildlife protected, and making our planet safe for us and future generations.

♥电影社团 Film Club

学生对电影制作艺术有着浓厚的兴趣。他们讨论 DIY 电影制作,分享自己的作品,以及如果有人正在考虑从事电影行业该考虑的事情。

Students have an interest in the art of film-making. They discuss DIY movie-making and share their works and what to consider if one is thinking about a career in the film industry.

♥辩论社团 Debating Club

辩论是一项有趣的、教育性的活动,是教师关注学生辩论兴趣的最佳途径。辩论社团在校园文化中起着主导作用,是一项很受欢迎的活动。

Debating is a fun and educational activity and is the best way for teachers to focus students' interest in debating. Debating club plays a leading part in the campus' culture. It is a very popular activity.

♥徒步旅行俱乐部 The Hiking Club

　　每年,越来越多的人在当地的徒步旅行俱乐部的帮助下走到户外享受乡村的美景。在英国,学生更可能遇到"爬山"或简单的"步行"俱乐部,而澳大利亚人则倾向于使用"丛林漫步"的称谓,新西兰人倾向于使用"徒步"的称谓。

Every year, more and more people head into the great outdoors to enjoy the beauty of the countryside with the help of their local hiking club. In England, students are more likely to come across "hill walking" or simply "walking" clubs, while Australians tend to use the term "bush walking" and New Zealanders tend to used the term "tramping".

♥橄榄球俱乐部 Rugby Club

　　英式橄榄球是19世纪上半叶起源于英格兰的一项接触式团体运动,它是一项风靡全球的体育运动,男女老少皆宜。橄榄球俱乐部的使命是弘扬比赛的精神。

Rugby is contact team sport which originated in England in the first half of the 19th century. It is a popular sport around the world, played by male and female players of all ages. The mission of rugby club is carrying forward the spirit of the game.

♥棒球社团 Baseball Club

在日本,棒球社团是最受欢迎的社团之一。棒球可以说是国民级的运动,从小学生到职业棒球联盟,各个年龄段都有棒球爱好者。

In Japan, baseball club is one of the most popular club. It can be said that baseball is a national sport. There are baseball fans of all ages ranging from elementary school students to professional baseball leagues.

少年观天下 Youth's View of the World

♥鹰嘴豆泥社团 Hummus Club

鹰嘴豆泥是英国人喜欢吃的一种酱,也是一种比较健康的食品,可以用来涂面包、蘸蔬菜、配烤肉等。这个社团会时不时地组织大家一起吃鹰嘴豆泥。

Hummus is a kind of sauce that British like to eat. It is also a kind of healthy food. It can be used to spread bread, dip in vegetables and roast meat. From time to time, this club organizes everybody to eat hummus.

♥连体衣社团 Kigu Club

连体衣社团又是什么呢？这就是一个穿着搞笑睡衣出去玩的借口。那些总说英国人古板严肃的人真要重新考虑一下了，因为这些可爱的学生可是十分认真的。

What is Kigu Club? Well, this is an excuse for going out to play in funny pajamas. Those who always say that the British are stereotyped and serious really need to reconsider, because these lovely students are very serious.

♥哑剧社团 Pantomime Club

没有对话或者歌唱，仅有夸张的肢体语言，这些学生们用精彩的演绎娱乐大众的同时，还让这项古老的艺术形式绽放出些许现代的光彩。

No dialogue or singing, only exaggerated body language is shown by these students to entertain the public with brilliant interpretation. They make this ancient art form blossom modern glory.

♥松鼠俱乐部 Squirrel Club

在美国密歇根州大学校园里面有很多非常大的松鼠。有的学生为此专门创办了一个松鼠俱乐部,每周有固定的同学来校园里面喂松鼠。这个俱乐部的同学每次喂松鼠的时候还会穿上"密歇根松鼠"字样的体恤,在校园中形成了一道独特的风景。

There are many large squirrels in the university campus of Michigan, USA. Some students set up a squirrel club to feed the squirrels on campus every week. Every time squirrels are fed, the students of this club wear "Michigan squirrels" T-shirts, creating a unique landscape in the campus.

活动体验馆 Activity Experience Pavilion

社团的教育理念是:关注人的全面发展,关注学生身心健康。

The purpose of club education is concerned with the whole person and with students' overall well-being.

同学们,你们知道为什么世界上各个国家的学校都组织这么多的社团吗?你觉得参加社团活动可以带来哪些好处呢? 请写下来。

Boys and girls, do you know why there are so many different kinds of clubs in schools all over the world and what benefit they bring to you? Please write them down.

通常的好处 General benefits	
交朋友，团队合作 Making friends, team work	
优雅的胜利或失败 Winning or losing graciously	
自信、荣耀、忠诚 Self-confidence, pride, loyalty	
建立人格 Character building	
道德决策 Moral decision making	
生活技能 Skills for life	
体育方面的好处 Benefits of sports	
身体健康——力量、柔韧性、耐力 Physical fitness—strength, flexibility, endurance	
心理健康——坚韧、思维敏捷、适应力强 Mental fitness—toughness, quick thinking, strong resilience	
社交技能——沟通 Social skills—communicating	
策略——在压力下正确决策 Strategy—making the right decisions under pressure	
领导技能 Leadership skills	

艺术方面的好处 Benefits of arts	
创新与表达 Innovation and expression	
新技能 New skills	
理解人类精神文明 Understanding the human spiritual civilization	
理解文化 Understanding cultures	
自信 Self-confidence	
交流 Communicating	
领导力 Leadership	
组织能力 Organizational skills	

第三节 研学之旅
Section 3　Research and Study Trip

📖 **身边小事　Little Things around Us**

　　金金激动地告诉湾湾,明天学校要组织大家去珠海机场航展馆参观学习。湾湾十分开心,他至今还回味上次在长隆海洋世界的研学活动,那可是意义非凡的一天呢!

　　Jinjin told Wanwan in excitement that they would go to see the Zhuhai Airport Museum the next day. Wanwan was happy to hear that. He still remembers the research and study activity in Chimelong Amusement Park last time, which was really a meaningful day!

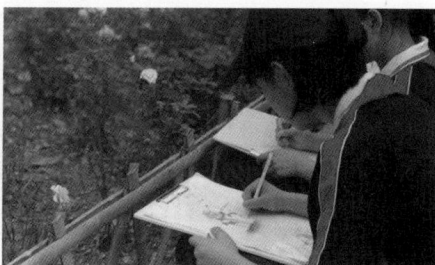

📖 **大家共言　Common Topic**

　　"读万卷书,行万里路",跨出这一步即是收获,行走这一路就是成长。同学们,你们学校给大家开展过什么样的研学活动呢?

　　"Read ten thousand books and walk ten thousands miles". Taking this step means gaining; walking this way is to grow. What kind of research and study activities has your school carried out for you?

少年观天下　Youth's View of the World

研学,是给孩子成长道路上一份见识的增长、一次视野的扩展。金湾区各学校组织学生通过集体旅行的方式走出校园,在与平常不同的生活中拓宽视野、丰富知识,加深与自然和文化的亲近感,增加对集体生活方式和社会公共道德的体验。

Research and study helps children to increase their knowledge and know more about the world. The schools in Jinwan District organize students to go out of the campus through group trips, and expand their horizons and enrich their knowledge in their lives, which are different from the usual ones. The activity draw students closer to nature and culture, increase the experience of collective life style and social public morality.

让我们来看看这些研学活动吧!

Let's have a look at these research and study activities!

♥生物研学 Biology Research and Study

猪笼草是濒危稀有的植物,在中国,保护珍稀野生猪笼草资源已刻不容缓。金海岸中学的华跃进老师通过科技活动小组来组织他的学生们研究和保护猪笼草,此举有助于学生了解猪笼草分布特征和生活习性,为改变猪笼草濒危现状提供科学途径。

Nepenthes mirabilis is an endangered and rare plant. In China, it is urgent to protect the rare and wild Nepenthes mirabilis resources. Mr. Hua Yuejin in Jinhaian

Middle School organizes his students to study and protect Nepenthes mirabilis by organizing scientific and technological activity groups. This activity helps students to understand its distribution characteristics and living habits. It provides a scientific way to change the endangered situation of Nepenthes mirabilis.

♥英语研学 English Research and Study

金海岸中学的学生去英国参加英语比赛和研学。

Students of Jinhaian Middle School went to England, took part in English competitions and research and study.

♥历史研学 History Research and Study

下图为刘昌言老师为学生讲解纪录片《三灶 1938》的拍摄过程,以及三灶的历史,使学生更加了解自己的成长之地。刘老师动员了很多学生帮他完成这项工作. 至纪录片完成, 参与翻译的学生有 20 多人. 学生们在此过程中收获颇多.

The following picture shows Mr. Liu Changyan explaining to the students the filming process of the documentary *Sanzao 1938*. He introduced the history of Sanzao to the students. This makes students learn more about the place where they grew up. Teacher Liu mobilized many students to help him to finish this work. By the time the documentary was completed, more than 20 students had participated in the translation. The students all gained a lot in the process.

♥创作研学 Creating Research and Study

初中生正在各图书馆制作手工。

Junior middle school students are doing handwork in libraries.

♥音乐研学 Music Research and Study

文化大合唱

cultural chorus

♥地理研学 Geography Research and Study

初中生们参加地理知识博览赛。

Junior middle school students participated in a geography competition.

♥航空研学 Aviation Research and Study

三灶中学的学生参观中航通用飞机有限责任公司。

The students in Sanzao Middle School visited China Aviation Industry General Aircraft Co. , Ltd. .

♥ 航模研学 Model Plane Research and Study

学生观看航模表演,航模设计者均为金湾区学生。

Students watched a model plane performance, the model plane designers are all students from Jinwan.

活动体验馆 Activity Experience Pavilion

同学们,你能设计一个研学活动吗？把你的设想写在下面吧。

Boys and girls, can you design a research and study activity? Write your ideas down.

时间 Time	地点 Place	人物 People	内容 Content	意义 Meaning

第四节 生 命 教 育
Section 4　Life Education

 身边小事　Little Things around Us

金金：什么声音,湾湾?

湾湾：学校正在进行消防演习呢! 当消防演习开始时,学生们将从大楼迅速撤出。

Jinjin: Wanwan, do you hear something?

Wanwan: There is a fire drill now at our school! When the fire drill starts, students will evacuate the building quickly.

 大家共言　Common Topic

老师：同学们,谁知道我们学校为什么要进行消防演习呢?

学生：生命就是希望,我们应该珍爱生命! 珍爱生命,关爱自己和他人……

Teacher: Who knows why there is a fire drill at our school?

Students: Life is hope, we should cherish life! Cherish life, is to care for ourselves and others...

少年观天下 Youth's View of the World

1968 年,美国的一位学者出版了《生命教育》一书,探讨关注人的生长发育与生命健康的教育真谛。近年来,日本、英国、中国等国家竭力倡导生命教育,各种学术团体纷纷建立。那么,什么是生命教育呢? 生命教育是在生命活动中进行教育,是为生命而进行教育。从事生命教育的肖敬认为生命教育是以生命为核心,以教育为手段,倡导认识生命、珍惜生命、尊重生命、爱护生命、享受生命、超越生命的一种提升生命质量、获得生命价值的教育活动。

In 1968, an American scholar published *Life Education*, which explores the need to pay attention to the truth of education in human growth and health. In recent years, Japan, the United Kingdom, China and other countries strive to promote life education, various academic groups have been established. So what is life education? Life education is education in life activity, education for life. Xiao Jing, who is engaged in life education, believes that life education is an educational activity with life as the core and education as the means to advocate recognizing life, cherishing life, respecting life, loving life, enjoying life and surpassing life to improve the quality of life and gain the value of life.

活动体验馆　Activity Experience Pavilion

你有哪些性格特征？

What personality traits do you have?

了解自己，做最好的自己。

Understand yourself, be your personal best.

生命的开始 The beginning of life	可爱的我 A lovely me	与众不同的我 A unique me	勇敢的我 A brave me	自信的我 A confident me

第二章　魅力世界
Chapter 2　Charming World

　　这个世界五彩缤纷、多姿多彩，让我们从美丽的金湾出发，开始一段游历世界各地风景名胜、体验风情各异的民俗文化、结识不同肤色朋友的旅行。

　　We are blessed with a world full of blazing colors and various beauty. Let's start from our fascinating hometown—Jinwan, and begin a journey, in which we can travel around places of interest of the world, experience varied folk cultures and meet friends from all corners of the world.

第一节　迷人风景
Section 1　Charming Scenery

📖 身边小事　Little Things around Us

暑假到了！爸爸和妈妈决定带金金和湾湾到美丽的珠海去玩。金金问："爸爸,珠海是个怎样的城市?"爸爸微笑着说："珠海是个美丽的海滨城市,有着柔软的沙滩、蓝蓝的海水和迷人的风景。"

Summer holiday is coming! Dad and mom, along with Jinjin and Wanwan decided to go to the beautiful city—Zhuhai. Jinjin asked: "Dad, what kind of city is Zhuhai?" Dad smiled and said: "Zhuhai is a beautiful seaside city, with soft sand, blue water and charming scenery."

珠海迷人的风景　Charming Scenery of Zhuhai

📖 大家共言　Common Topic

孩子们,大自然为我们创造了什么迷人的风景?

Children, what charming scenery has nature created for us?

草原
Prairies

山川
Mountains and rivers

湖泊
Lakes

沙漠和森林
Deserts and forests

少年观天下 Youth's View of the World

几十亿年过去了,大自然为我们美丽的地球创造了许多壮观的自然景观,让我们一起来看看世界的自然奇观吧!

As billions of years passed, nature has created many spectacular natural landscapes for our beautiful planet. Let's take a look at the natural wonders of the world.

科罗拉多大峡谷位于美国亚利桑那州,是地球上七大自然奇观之一。在过去600万年里,大峡谷在科罗拉多河的作用下被"雕刻"而成。科罗拉多大峡谷以其石灰岩、页岩和砂石的多色带而闻名。

The Grand Canyon of Colorado, one of the Seven Natural Wonders of the world, is located in Arizona, USA. For the past six million years, it has been "craved" with the power of Colorado River. The Grand Canyon of Colorado is famous for its multihued bands of limestones, shales and sandstones.

科罗拉多大峡谷 **The Grand Canyon of Colorado**

位于南半球的大堡礁,形成于中新世时期,距今已有 2 500 万年的历史。它是世界上最大的珊瑚礁群,有 2 900 个珊瑚礁岛,自然景观非常独特。

Located in the Southern hemisphere, the Great Barrier Reef come into being during the Miocene period with a long history of 25 million years. Covering 2, 900 coral reef islands, it is the world's largest coral reef group as well as its special natural landscape.

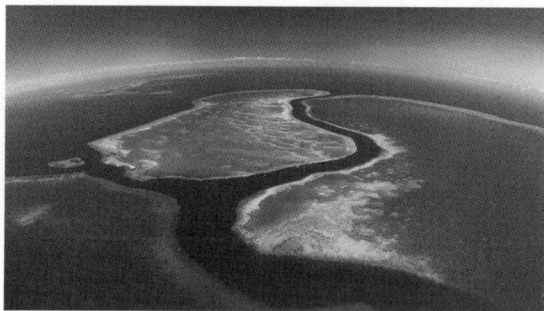

大堡礁　**The Great Barrier Reef**

帕里库廷火山是位于墨西哥米却肯州西部的一座火山,因在帕里库廷村附近而得名。它是北美洲最年轻的火山,也是世界上较年轻的火山,被许多人称为世界七大自然奇观之一。

Paricutin Volcano, located in the western part of Michoacan, Mexicó, is named after the village of Paricutin. It is the youngest volcano in North America and is also a relatively young volcano in the world. Many people call it one of the seven natural wonders of the world.

帕里库廷火山　**Paricutin Volcano**

伊瓜苏大瀑布是世界上最宽的瀑布,位于阿根廷和巴西两国边境。"伊瓜苏"在南美洲土著居民瓜拉尼人的语言中是"伟大的水"的意思。1984 年,伊瓜苏大瀑布被联合国教科文组织列为世界自然遗产。

Cataratas del Iguazú, the widest waterfall in the world, is located on the border between Argentina and Brazil. In the language of the native people of South America, "Iguazú" means "great water". In 1894, it was listed as the World Natural Heritage Site by UNESCO.

伊瓜苏大瀑布　Cataratas del Iguazú

桂林地处中国广西壮族自治区东北部,是广西最大空港,属山地丘陵地区。这里为典型的喀斯特岩溶地貌,遍布全市的石灰岩经过亿万年的风化侵蚀,形成了千峰环立、一水抱城、洞奇石美的独特景观。

Located in the northeastern part of Guangxi Zhuang Autonomous Region of China, Guilin is the largest airport in Guangxi and is a mountainous hilly area. It is a typical "Karst" landform. Its limestone that spreads throughout the city has been weathered and eroded for millions of years, forming thousands of peaks, which makes Guilin a unique landscape of strange and beautiful cave, stone as well as water.

桂林　Guilin

活动体验馆　Activity Experience Pavilion

请你搜集资料,向同学介绍一下你家乡的迷人风景,包括它的具体地理位置、起源、迷人之处、历史等。

Please search for the information about your hometown's charming scenery and share them with your classmates. The information may include its location, origin, attractions, history and so on.

家乡最美的风景是_____

My hometown's most charming scenery is _____

地理位置 Location	
起源 Origin	
迷人之处 Attractions	
历史 History	
……	

第二节 各异文化
Section 2 Different Cultures

身边小事 **Little Things around Us**

　　就要放暑假了,同学们都计划着出去旅游,有想到国内其他省旅游的,有想去欧洲或者美国旅游的,金金和湾湾也在商量要去哪里。金金说:"我想去俄罗斯,我在电视上看到那里的景色挺漂亮的。"湾湾说:"妈妈说要带我去日本,因为我非常喜欢日本的动漫,而且想看看富士山。"

　　Summer vacation is coming. The students are planning to travel, some want to go to other provinces in China, some want to go to Europe or the United States. Jinjin and Wanwan also discuss where to go. "I want to go to Russia, because I saw it on TV that it was beautiful, " Jinjin said. "My mother said she would take me to Japan because I like Japanese anime very much and would like to see Mount Fuji, " Wanwan said.

　　这时,英语老师刚好经过教室,她听见大家的计划和议论,笑着对大家说:"各位同学,如果你们要出去旅游,一定要先了解一下目的地的文化,如果你们不懂当地的文化,会闹出笑话甚至会产生误会的。"

　　At this time, the English teacher just passed the classroom. When she heard students' plans, she said with a smile to them: "If you want to travel, you must first understand the culture of the destination. If you don't understand the local culture, you will make jokes or even be misunderstood. "

大家共言 **Common Topic**

　　文化是人类所创造的精神财富,那么,文化具体是指什么呢?

　　Culture is the spiritual wealth created by mankind. So, what does culture specifically mean?

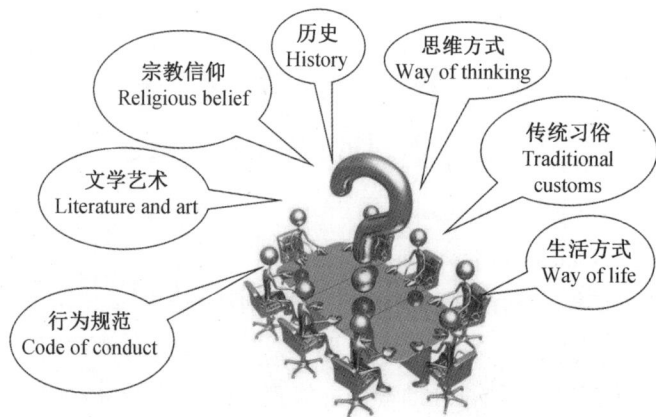

宗教信仰 Religious belief
历史 History
思维方式 Way of thinking
传统习俗 Traditional customs
文学艺术 Literature and art
生活方式 Way of life
行为规范 Code of conduct

少年观天下 Youth's View of the World

让我们一起来看看世界各地多姿多彩的文化吧！

Let's take a look at the colorful cultures of the world!

♥亚洲文化 Asian Culture

亚洲意为"太阳升起的地方"。它是世界七大洲中面积最大、人口最多的一个洲。亚洲以黄种人为主,种族、民族构成最为复杂,全洲民族、种族共有 1 000多个,尤以南亚为甚。亚洲还是世界三大宗教——佛教、伊斯兰教和基督教的发祥地。举世闻名的四大文明古国亚洲占据三席,对世界文化的发展有着重要的影响。

Asia means "the place where the sun rises". It is the largest and most populous of the seven continents in the world. Asia is dominated by the yellow race, with the most complex racial and ethnic composition. There are more than 1, 000 ethnic groups across the continent, especially in South Asia. Asia is also the birthplace of the world's three major religions—Buddhism, Islam and Christianity. The world-famous four ancient civilizations, Asia, occupy three seats and have a significant impact on the development of world culture.

1. 日本 Japan

日本独特的地理条件和悠久的历史,孕育了别具一格的日本文化。樱花、和服、武士、清酒、神道教构成了日本传统的两个方面——菊花与剑。日本的官方语言是日语。

Japan's unique geographical conditions and long history have given birth to a unique Japanese culture. Cherry blossoms, kimono, samurai, sake and Shinto constitute two aspects of Japanese tradition—chrysanthemums and swords. The official language of Japan is Japanese.

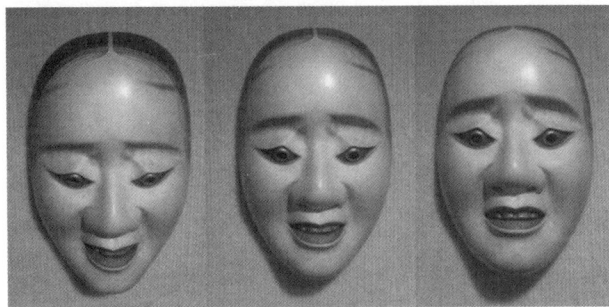

"能"面具　Mask of Energy

2. 印度 India

99%以上的印度居民有宗教信仰。印度的主要宗教按教徒多少依次为印度教、伊斯兰教、基督教、锡克教、耆那教、佛教和袄教等。印度的国树为菩提树,国鸟为蓝孔雀,国花为荷花,这些均与印度人的宗教信仰有关。印度共有1 652种语言和方言,当地宪法规定了18种语言为联邦官方语言,还规定英语为行政和司法用语。

More than 99% of Indians are religious. The major religions in India are Hinduism, Islam, Christianity, Sikhism, Jainism, Buddhism and Zoroastrianism in the order of the number of the believers. The national tree of India is Bodhi Tree, the national bird is blue peacock, and the national flower is lotus, which are all related to the religious beliefs of Indians. India has a total of 1, 652 languages and dialects. The Constitution stipulates that 18 languages are the official languages of the Federation, and English is also an administrative and judicial language.

摩诃菩提寺　**Mahabodhi Temple**

圣城瓦拉纳西　**Holy City Varanasi**

泰姬陵　**Taj Mahal**

3. 巴基斯坦 Pakistan

巴基斯坦意为"圣洁的土地""清真之国"。95%以上的居民信奉伊斯兰教，巴基斯坦是一个多民族伊斯兰国家。官方语言为乌尔都语。巴基斯坦男人穿白色长裤和各式上衣，妇女按伊斯兰教要求进行装扮，用长袍、长裤和罩衫遮住全部身体。这里绝对禁酒，包括啤酒，还有无醇的酒，但不禁烟。

Pakistan means "holy land" and "land of halal". More than 95% of residents believe in Islam. Pakistan is a multi-ethnic Islamic country. The official language is Urdu. Pakistani men wear white trousers and various tops. Women dress up in accordance with Islamic requirements and cover their bodies with robes, trousers and blouses. Alcohol is absolutely prohibited here, including beer and alcohol-free wine, but smoking is allowed.

清真寺　The Mosque

♥北美洲文化 North American Culture

北美洲位于西半球北部,是世界第三大洲,为世界经济第二发达的大洲。通用语言是英语,其次是西班牙语、法语、荷兰语、印第安语等。大部分居民是欧洲移民的后裔,居民主要信仰新教和天主教。

Located in the northern western hemisphere, North America is the third continent in the world and the second most developed continent in the world economy. The universal language is English, followed by Spanish, French, Dutch, Indian, etc. Most of the inhabitants are descendants of European immigrants, and the residents mainly believe in Protestantism and Catholicism.

1. 美国 The United States

个人主义是美国文化的核心。美国人崇尚个人至上、自我奋斗,深信个人尊严,为自己而生活,讲究个人特色,追求自我表现。因此,信奉个人主义的美国人把自己的年龄、婚姻状况、体重、收入、宗教信仰以及个人生活,都看作个人隐私。绝大多数的美国人信奉宗教,以基督教为主。

Individualism is the core of American culture. Americans advocate personal supremacy, self-strengthening, conviction of personal dignity, living for themselves, paying attention to personal characteristics, and pursuing self-expression. Therefore, Americans who believe in individualism regard their age, marital status, weight, income, religious beliefs, and personal life as personal privacy. The vast majorities of Americans believe in religion and are predominantly Christian.

美国是一个多民族的大熔炉，不仅有原住民印第安人，还有欧洲、非洲移民的后裔，以及拉丁美洲和亚洲人的后代，每年有数十万来自世界各地的合法或非法的移民涌入美国。各种文化和宗教信仰在不同的种族之间不断交融，但是隐形的种族歧视依然存在。

The United States is a melting pot of multi-ethnic people including not only aboriginal Indians, but also descendants of European and African immigrants, and descendants of Latin American and Asian people. Hundreds of thousands of legal or illegal immigrants from all over the world come in the United States every year. Various cultures and religious beliefs continue to blend between different races, but invisible racial discrimination still exists.

迪士尼乐园　Disneyland

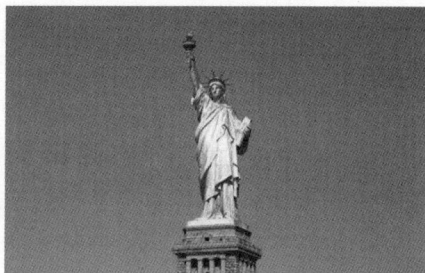

自由女神像　The Statue of Liberty

2. 加拿大 Canada

加拿大位于北美洲北端，英联邦国家之一，素有"枫叶之国"的美誉，其首都是渥太华。官方语言有英语和法语两种，是典型的双语国家。加拿大文化多元，同时是一个移民大国，还是一个崇尚个性解放、个人隐私的国家。不同的文化，无论其强弱，都在加拿大这片自由的土地上得以独立完整地保持自己的特色，而不被同化或消亡。

Canada, located in the northern part of North America, is one of the Commonwealth countries and is known as the "Maple Leaf Country". The capital is Ottawa. The official language is English and French, and is a typical bilingual country. Canadian culture is diverse, and it is also a big immigrant country. It is also a country that advocates individual liberation and personal privacy. Different cultures, regardless of their strengths and weaknesses, are able to maintain their own characteristics in this free land without being assimilated or dying.

枫叶之国 Maple Leaf Country

白求恩故居 Former Residence of Bethune

♥拉丁美洲文化 Latin American Culture

拉丁美洲是指美国以南的美洲地区。在历史上,这一地区主要是拉丁语系的西班牙和葡萄牙等国的殖民地,故称拉丁美洲。种族主要是印欧混血种人和黑白混血种人,次为黑人、印第安人和白种人。拉丁美洲国家所使用的语言有西班牙语、葡萄牙语、英语、法语、荷兰语以及多种印第安语等。拉丁美洲国家信奉同一个宗教——罗马天主教。

Latin America refers to the Americas region south of the United States. Historically, this region is mainly a Latin American colony of Spain and Portugal, so it is called Latin America. The race is mainly Indian-European mixed-race and black-and-white mixed-race, followed by blacks, Indians and Caucasians. The languages spoken in Latin American countries are Spanish, Portuguese, English, French, Dutch, and a variety of Indian languages. Latin American countries believe in the same religion—Roman Catholicism.

1. 巴西 Brazil

巴西是拉丁美洲最大的国家,巴西的文化具有多重民族的特性,作为一个民族大熔炉,有来自欧洲、非洲、亚洲等地的移民。巴西的官方语言是葡萄牙语。足球是巴西人文化生活的主流运动,因此,巴西享有"足球王国"的美誉。巴西人浪漫而热情,被称为"桑巴的国度"。巴西人在社交场合通常以拥抱或者亲吻作为见面礼节,只有在十分正式的活动中,他们才相互握手。除此之外,巴西人还有一些独特的见面礼,例如握拳礼、贴面礼和沐浴礼等。

As the largest country in Latin America, Brazil has a multi-ethnic culture. As a melting pot, it has immigrants from Europe, Africa, Asia and other places. The official language of Brazil is Portuguese. Football is the mainstream sport of Brazilian cultural life, so Brazil enjoys the reputation of the "kingdom of football". Brazilians are romantic and passionate and are known as the land of the samba. Brazilians usually use hugs or kisses as a courtesy in social situations. Only in very formal activities, they shake hands with each other. In addition, the Brazilians also have some unique meeting rituals, for example, fist ritual, bisous and bathing ceremony.

桑巴舞　Samba

贴面礼　Bisous

2. 秘鲁 Peru

秘鲁是拉丁美洲西部的一个国家,官方语言为西班牙语,一些地区通用克丘亚语、艾马拉语和其他30多种印第安语。96%的居民信奉天主教。各民族文化传统的融合在艺术、饮食、文学和音乐等领域形成了多元的表达方式。

Peru is a country in western Latin America. The official language is Spanish. Some regions are common Quechua, Aymara and more than 30 other Indian languages. 96% of the residents believe in Catholicism. The integration of various national cultural traditions has created diverse expressions in the fields of art, food, literature and music.

斗牛

Bullfighting

马丘比丘古城

The Ancient City of Machu Picchu

♥大洋洲文化 Oceanian Culture

大洋洲陆地总面积约897万平方千米,是世界上最小的一个大洲。除南极洲外,它是世界上人口最少的一个大洲。大洋洲以基督教、原始宗教信仰为主。原始宗教信仰者分布广泛,另外还有伊斯兰教、印度教、佛教、犹太教等其他宗教信徒。大洋洲绝大部分居民使用英语。

The total land area of Oceania is about 8.97 million square kilometers, which is the smallest continent in the world. With the exception of Antarctica, it is the world's least populated continent. Oceania is dominated by Christianity and primitive religious beliefs. Primitive believers are widely distributed, and there are other religions such as Islam, Hinduism, Buddhism and Judaism. Most people in Oceania use English.

1. 澳大利亚 Australia

澳大利亚拥有很多独特的动植物和自然景观,是典型的移民国家,奉行多元文化,被社会学家喻为"民族的拼盘"。英语是澳大利亚的官方语言,但同时还有很多其他的语言在这里使用。澳大利亚是一个宗教自由的国家,各种宗教信仰并存,包括基督教、天主教、印度教、犹太教、伊斯兰教和佛教等。

Australia has many unique fauna, flora and natural landscapes. It is a typical immigrant country, pursuing multiculturalism and being referred to by sociologists as a "national platter". English is the official language of Australia, but there are many other languages used here. Australia is a country of religious freedom with various religious beliefs. Christianity, Catholicism, Hinduism, Judaism, Islam and Buddhism coexist in this country.

阿德莱德艺术节 The Adelaide Festival

悉尼歌剧院　Sydney Opera House

2. 新西兰 New Zealand

新西兰是南太平洋的一个国家,是大洋洲最美丽的国家之一,总计约有30%的国土为保护区。它拥有3项世界遗产、14个国家公园、3座海洋公园、数百座自然保护区和生态区。新西兰规定了3种官方语言,分别是英语、毛利语、新西兰手语。新西兰人见面和告别时均行握手礼。

New Zealand is a country in the South Pacific and one of the most beautiful countries in Oceania. A total of about 30% of the country is the nature reserve. It has 3 world heritage sites, 14 national parks, 3 marine parks, hundreds of nature reserves and ecological zones. New Zealand defines 3 official languages: English, Maori, New Zealand Sign Language. New Zealanders shake hands with each other when they meet and say goodbye.

毛利战舞　Maori War Dance

活动体验馆　Activity Experience Pavilion

我们在上面已经了解了四大洲的不同文化,那么你肯定会有疑问了:为什

么没有介绍我们熟悉的英国、法国、俄罗斯和埃及等国家呢？不要着急,留给你
自己去查找资料来补充。

We have already seen the different cultures of the four continents, and now you
will definitely have doubts: Why is there no introduction about the United Kingdom,
France, Russia and Egypt that we are familiar with? Don't worry, now it's time for
you to find more information by yourself.

欧洲和非洲文化　**European and African culture**

国家 Country	内容 Contents					
	语言 Language	民族 National	宗教 Religion	节日 Festival	习惯与习俗 Habits and customs	礼仪 Etiquette
英国 United Kingdom						
法国 France						
德国 Germany						
俄罗斯 Russia						
希腊 Greece						
埃及 Egypt						
南非 South Africa						

第三节 多彩民族
Section 3 Colorful Ethnic Groups

身边小事 Little Things around Us

春节期间,金金的美国朋友瑞秋来金湾游玩。她对中国的传统节日很感兴趣,于是金金向她介绍了中国的节日。

Rachel, Jinjin's American friend, paid a visit to Jinwan in the Spring Festival. She is interested in traditional festivals in China, thus Jinjin introduced Chinese festivals to her.

大家共言 Common Topic

西方最重要的节日是圣诞节,那中国呢?
The most important festival in the west is Christmas. What about China?

春节期间你们有哪些庆祝活动?
What kind of elebrations do you have in the Spring Festival?

春节是中国最重要的节日,大家都会回家团聚。
The Spring Festival is the most important festival in China when all family members get together.

所有家庭成员一起吃晚饭,拜访亲友。
All family members eat dinner together, visit relatives and friends.

少年观天下 Youth's View of the World

中国的传统节日形式多样、内容丰富,是我们中华民族悠久历史文化的一个组成部分。

Traditional Chinese festivals are abundant in forms and content, which are part of the long history and culture of the Chinese nation.

首先，让我们看看中国多彩的传统节日。

First of all, let's have a look at the colorful traditional festivals in China.

新年来临之际，人们开始装饰干净的房子，让它充满欢乐和节日气氛。在屋内外都能看到汉字"福"（寓意为祝福或幸福）、红灯笼和红剪纸。此外，大人们给孩子们发红包，带他们看龙狮舞。

Before the New Year comes, people begin decorating their clean rooms featuring an atmosphere of rejoicing and festivity. The Chinese character "fu" (meaning blessing or happiness), red lanterns, red paper-cuttings can be seen in and out of the houses. Additionally, adults give money in red envelopes to kids, and take them to watch dragon and lion dances.

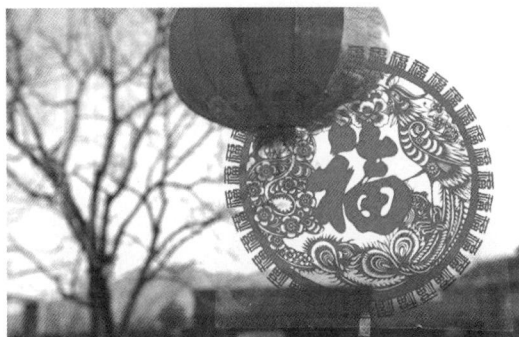

红灯笼和红剪纸　**Red Lanterns, Red Paper-Cuttings**

龙狮舞　**Dragon and Lion Dances**

春节刚过,就迎来了元宵节。人们全家团聚,共吃元宵、燃灯放焰、喜猜灯谜。

The Lantern Festival comes just after the Spring Festival. People have a family reunion and celebrate the festival. They eat special sweet dumplings, light lanterns and fireworks as well as guess the lantern riddles.

元宵节 **The Lantern Festival**

龙舟节,又称端午节。千百年来,人们在这个节日里吃粽子(将糯米饭用竹叶或芦苇叶包裹成一个金字塔),赛龙舟。

The Dragon Boat Festival is also called the Duanwu Festival. For thousands of years, the festival has been marked by eating zongzi (glutinous rice wrapped to form a pyramid using bamboo or reed leaves) and racing dragon boats.

粽子 **Zongzi**

赛龙舟 **Racing Dragon Boats**

七夕节是中国传统节日中最具浪漫色彩的一个节日。象征忠贞爱情的牛郎织女的传说,一直在民间流传。

Qiqiao Festival is the most romantic Chinese traditional festivals. The legend of the cowherd and the weaver girl symbolizes loyalty and love, which has been circulating among the people.

七夕节　**Qiqiao Festival**

中秋节这天,家人团聚,共同观赏象征丰裕、和谐和幸运的圆月。大人通常会喝一杯清热的中国茶,品尝多种月饼,而孩子们则提着灯笼跑来跑去。

Mid-Autumn Festival is a happy time for family members to congregate and enjoy the full moon—an auspicious symbol of abundance, harmony and luck. Adults will usually indulge in fragrant mooncakes of many varieties with a good cup of piping hot Chinese tea, while the children run around with their lanterns.

赏月　**Admire Moon**

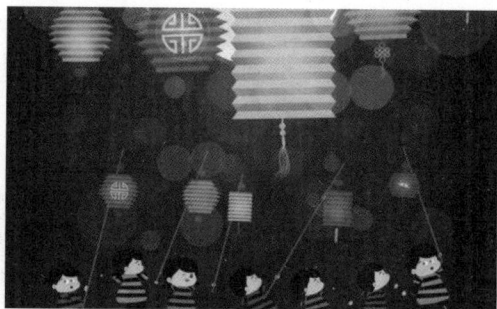

点灯笼 **Light Lantern**

除了中国的传统节日,西方国家也有着丰富多彩、各具特色的节日。

In addition to traditional Chinese festivals, western countries also have rich and colorful festivals with their own characteristics.

复活节是西方的重要节日,象征着重生与希望。复活节的主要特色是赠送礼物。鲜花、复活蛋、复活兔、羔羊都是复活节的象征物。

Easter is one of the most significant western festivals, symbolizing rebirth and hope. The main feature of Easter is the giving of gifts. Flowers, Easter eggs, Easter Bunny, lambs are all symbols of Easter.

复活蛋、复活兔 **Easter Eggs, Easter Bunny**

感恩节是美国和加拿大共有的节日,原意是为了感谢上天赐予的好收成,后来人们常在这一天感谢他人。每逢感恩节这一天,家家户户都要吃火鸡。

Thanksgiving Day is the shared festival between United States and Canada. It was meant to thank God for the good harvest. Later, people often express their thanks to others on this day. On Thanksgiving Day, every family has to eat turkey.

感恩节　**Thanksgiving Day**

火鸡　**Turkey**

活动体验馆　Activity Experience Pavilion

同学们,你们知道中西方还有哪些传统节日? 下面是头脑风暴图,请与同学讨论并列举出更多的中西方节日。

Boys and girls, do you know other traditional festivals in China and western countries? Here below are the brainstorming charts. Please discuss and list more Chinese and western festivals with your classmates.

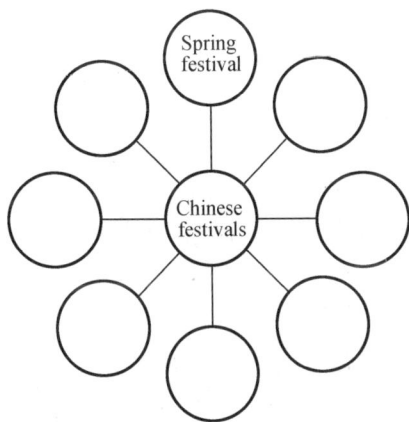

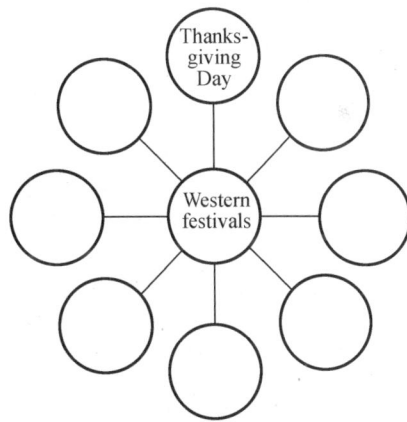

第四节 共爱家园

Section 4　Loving Home Together

身边小事　**Little Things around Us**

金金:最近有好几次台风登陆。

湾湾:是啊,好讨厌,台风一来学校里就积水泛滥。

金金:不用担心了,学校正在进行海绵工程,以后不会再有积水了。

湾湾:噢,太棒了! 这让我们的学校更加安全了。

Jinjin: There'll be several typhoons recently.

Wanwan: Yes, I hate them! Whenever a typhoon hits, it floods the roads and playground in our school.

Jinjin: Never mind! The sponge engineering is going well in our school. It won't flood again.

Wanwan: Oh, that's great! Our school becomes much safer.

大家共言 Common Topic

地球是适合我们生活的唯一星球,如何提高人们的意识和责任感来保护我们宝贵的家园呢?

The earth is the unique planet suitable for us to live on. How can we raise people's awareness and responsibility of protecting our precious home?

少年观天下 Youth's View of the World

全世界都在不遗余力地保护我们的家园,各种纪念日因此产生。

The whole world spares no effort to protect our home, thus all kinds of memorial days are set.

世界环境日促进全球环境意识,提高政府对环境问题的关注并采取行动。

World Environment Day aims to promote global environmental awareness, raise government's attention on environmental problems and take actions.

世界水日的宗旨是唤起公众的节水意识,加强对水资源的保护。

World Water Day aims to awaken people's water saving consciousness and strengthen water resources protection.

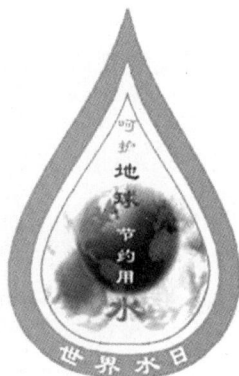

世界地球日旨在提高民众对现有环境问题的意识,并动员民众参与到环保运动中,通过低碳生活,改善地球的整体环境。

World Earth Day aims to raise people's awareness of the present environmental problems and encourage people to participate in the campaign of environment protection by means of low-carbon life to improve the overall environment of the earth.

世界动物日是每年的 10 月 4 日,号召人们保护动物、善待动物。

World Animal Day is On October 4 each year, it calls on people to protect animals and treat them well.

世界森林日旨在唤起世界各国更加重视保护和发展森林资源，推进全球性植树运动，积极维护生态安全，共同应对气候变化。

World Forest Day is aimed to raise the awareness of countries in the world to pay more attention to protecting and developing forest resources, to promote the global tree planting campaign, to safeguard ecological safety actively and to tackle climate change together.

活动体验馆　Activity Experience Pavilion

珠海有一位名为梁华坤的乐观爱笑的大学生农民企业家，他就是著名的"鸟叔"，创立了远近闻名的生态养殖基地。他倾尽所有，自己甘愿省吃俭用，十年投入了两千多万元，在自承包的千亩良田中划出三百多亩用作珠三角最大的雀鸟保育基地。现在园里有近百种雀鸟，数量达十万只。他是自然生态环境保育的先锋!

In Zhuhai, Liang Huakun, a college student farmer and entrepreneur who likes to laugh and be optimistic, the well-known "Uncle Bird". He founded the famous ecological breeding base with all that he has. More than 20 million yuan has been put into the base during ten years while he leads a simple and frugal life. In the base covering the area of 300 mu live over a hundred kinds of birds and the number adds up to one hundred thousand. He is a recognized pioneer of natural ecological conservation.

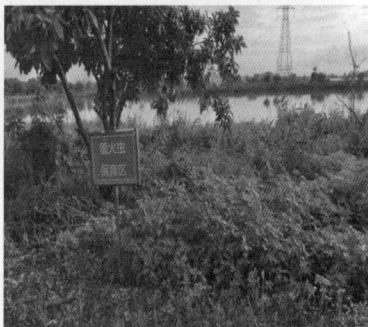

读了"鸟叔"的故事,金金和湾湾不仅计划去参观这个基地,还提出保护地球的建议。

After reading Uncle Bird's story, Jinjin and Wanwan are not only intended to pay a visit to the base, but also put forward some suggestions for protecting the earth.

第三章 国际公民
Chapter 3 A Global Citizen

　　随着科技的发展,世界各国人民的交往日益频繁,人们之间的关系更加紧密,我们分享着相同的电视节目、时装和产品,为全球化带来的美好生活而欢呼。富强起来的中国老百姓开始走出国门到国外旅游、学习,外国人出现在中国街头也不是什么新鲜事。虽然同住一个"地球村",但我们这个"村"很庞大,在这个"村"里有很多种族,有黄色人种、白色人种、黑色人种和棕色人种,各国和各地区风俗文化迥异。为了更好地交流,我们需要了解各国的文明礼仪,与外国友人建立和谐平等的关系;为了让我们生活的这个"地球村"更加宜居,我们需要重视环保、关注公益。

　　With the development of science and technology, the people in the world communicate more and more frequently, and the relationship between them is closer. We share the same TV programs, fashion and products, and cheer for the beautiful life brought by globalization. The wealthy Chinese people began to go abroad to travel and study. It is not a new thing for foreigners to appear on the streets of China. Although we live in a "global village", our "village" is very large. There are many races in the "village", including yellow race, white race, black race and brown race. The customs and cultures of different countries and regions are different. To communicate well, we need to understand the etiquette of each country and establish a harmonious and equal relationship with foreign friends. In order to make our "global village" living more habitable, we need to pay attention to environmental protection and public welfare.

第一节 文 明 礼 仪
Section 1　Good Manners

身边小事　Little Things around Us

　　珠海航展就快到了。来自世界各地的友人会共享这次航空盛宴。金金说："我很高兴能成为一名志愿者。但是我应该怎么样和不同国家的人打招呼才合适呢?"湾湾说:"保持微笑和热情。"

　　Zhuhai Airshow is coming soon. People from all over the world will come and celebrate this aviation feast together. Jinjin said: "I am glad to become a volunteer. But how should I greet people from different countries in the right way?" Wanwan replies: "Keep smiling and be passionate!"

大家共言　Common Topic

　　同学们,虽然不同的地方有不同的礼仪,但是你能想出世界上被一致认可的文明礼仪有哪些吗?

　　Boys and girls, although there are different manners in different places, can you think of some manners that are commonly considered good across cultures?

Punctuality	准时 Be on time!
	微笑 Smile!
	穿着得体 Get properly dressed!
Say PLEASE	使用文明用语 Use polite language!

少年观天下　Youth's View of the World

同学们,珠海航展每两年举行一次,届时世界各国都会在珠海展示他们最雄厚的航空航天实力。当你遇见外国人的时候,你知道如何与他们打招呼吗?

Boys and girls, Zhuhai Airshow is held every two years. At that time, a lot of countries in the world will show their most abundant aerospace strength in Zhuhai. When you meet foreigners, do you know how to greet them?

为了更好地展示东道主城市和中国青少年的形象,接下来让我们一起学习不同国家的一些文明礼仪吧!

In order to better display the image of the host city and the young people of

China, let's learn some manners of different countries together.

♥握手礼仪 Shaking Hands

握手是一种很常用的礼节,一般用在见面、离别、祝贺等场景。它是现在社会大多数国家相见时最常用的礼节,广泛运用于政要、商要和普通百姓之间。

Shaking hands is a common etiquette, it's usually used to meet, leave and congratulate each other. It is the most common etiquette in most countries in modern society. It is widely used between politicians, businessmen and ordinary people.

♥接吻礼仪 Kissing

接吻常见于西方、东欧、阿拉伯国家,是亲人和亲密的朋友之间表示亲昵、慰问、爱抚的一种礼仪,通常是在受礼者脸上或额上亲一下。

Kissing is commonly used in western or eastern European and Arab countries. It is a custom for relatives and close friends to show their close relationship, condole or caress. People always give the recipient a kiss on the cheek or forehead.

♥ 拥抱礼仪 Hug

拥抱是在欧美、中东及南美洲的常见礼节，一般用于熟人和朋友之间，是一种比较亲密的见面礼仪。

Hug is a common etiquette in Europe, the United States, the Middle East and South America. It's generally used between relatives or friends, It is a more intimate meeting manner.

♥ 鞠躬礼仪 Bow

这种礼仪常见于日本和韩国，属于比较普及的礼仪。

Bowing is usually used in Japan and South Korea. It is a very common manner.

活动体验馆　**Activity Experience Pavilion**

　　同学们,对于不同国家的文明礼仪你们都了解清楚了吗？下面让我们一起来为这些国家寻找正确的文明礼仪吧！加油！

　　Boys and girls, are you familiar with different kinds of manners in the world? Let's try to find the right manners for these countries. Come on!

In Japan （　　）

In India （　　）

In China （　　）

In Netherlands （　　）

In North Pole （　　）

①

②

③

④

⑤

第二节 关注公益
Section 2 Public Welfare

📖 **身边小事 Little Things around Us**

金金:今天我们中学迎来了一群大学生。

湾湾:我知道。他们来自吉林大学珠海学院青年志愿者协会,是吉林大学珠海学院协会的大哥哥和大姐姐。

Jinjin: We saw a group of university students in our middle school today.

Wanwan: I know who they are. They are the elder brothers and sisters of the Youth Volunteer Association of Zhuhai College of Jilin University.

吉林大学珠海学院青年志愿者协会
Youth Volunteer Association of Zhuhai College of Jilin University

金金:他们有关爱农民工子女、扶残助残、探访孤寡老人等形式多样的志愿活动。

湾湾:真棒!学校门口宣传栏上有很多他们做公益活动的照片,我们一起去看看吧。

Jinjin: They have various forms of volunteer activities—Caring for the migrant workers' children, helping disabled people, visiting the lonely old people.

Wanwan: How great they are! There are a lot of pictures in the school publicity column when volunteers did good deeds. Let's go and have a look.

中国航展志愿服务　**China Airshow Volunteer Service**

清洗风扇活动　**Cleaning Fan Activities**

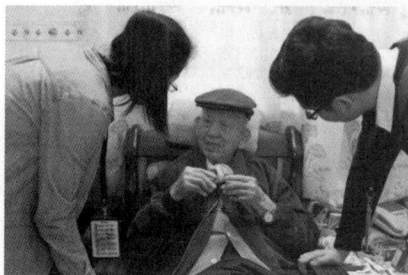

探望孤寡老人活动　**Visiting the Lonely Old People**

大家共言 Common Topic

金金:什么是公益？你知道吗？

湾湾:从字面的意思来看,"公益"是为了公众的利益。你的一份爱心能惠及很多人。

金金:公益活动的内容包括哪些？

湾湾:有很多啊。比如劝导路人正确过马路,协助警察维护好路口的交通秩序;捡废品去卖,将钱捐给需要的人;慰问敬老院的老人;关心孤儿院的小孩;为父母洗脚,问候父母等。

Jinjin: What is public welfare? Do you know?

Wanwan: Public welfare is literally for the benefits of the public. Your love can benefit a lot of people.

Jinjin: What are the contents of public welfare activities?

Wanwan: There are so many activities. For example, persuading passers-by how to cross the road correctly, assisting police in maintaining traffic order at junctions; picking up the waste and selling it and donating money to the people in need; visiting old people; caring for children in the orphanage; washing feet for parents, visiting parents and so on.

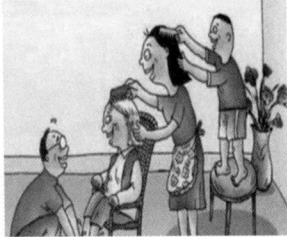

金金:活动真是丰富多彩。还有很多能够称之为"公益"的事,你知道吗?

湾湾:我当然知道! 赞助教育事业的公益活动,这样的活动不仅有利于教育事业的发展,也利于树立社会组织关心社会教育的良好形象。

Jinjin: Activities are rich and colorful. There are many other things to be called "public welfare". Do you know?

Wanwan: Of course, I know! Public welfare activities for sponsoring education. It is not only conducive to the development of education, but also helps to establish a good image of social organizations concerned about social education.

图书捐赠活动　**Books Donation Activities**

图书馆捐赠活动　**Library Donation Activities**

学习用品捐赠活动　**Learning Goods Donation Activities**

少年观天下　Youth's View of the World

同学们,不同的国家有不同的社会公益活动。现在,让我们一起来了解国外的一些公益活动吧!

Boys and girls, different countries have different social public welfare activities. Now, Let us take a look at some public welfare activities abroad!

♥土耳其 Turkey

土耳其动物爱护组织(Pugedon)设计出一款独特的饮料瓶回收器。这款设备看起来和普通的售卖机没有什么区别,但只要大家将饮料瓶投入其中,机器就会放出饲料,流浪动物们就可以饱餐一顿。

Turkey animal care organization (Pugedon) designed a unique beverage bottle recovery device. The device looks like the same as ordinary vending machines. But when you throw the beverage bottle in it, the machine will feed out so the stray animals can have a good meal.

♥西班牙 Spain

你知道狼人吗? 就是半狼半人的妖。西班牙的帕金森协会组织人员让那些患有帕金森病的西班牙老年人穿上狼人的衣服上街去宣传,他们逢人便说自己是"前狼人"。狼人从电影来到现实,为公益而活。快来拯救"前狼人"吧!

Do you know the Werewolf? It is half human and half wolf. Organization of Parkinson Association of Spain arrange for the Parkinson's elder wear the Werewolf's clothes, go to the streets to publicize that they are "former Werewolves". Werewolves come out from film to reality, and live for the public welfar. Come and save the "former Werewolf"!

♥美国 America

美国 ALS 协会进行了一项风靡全球的公益活动——"冰桶挑战"，这是在体验一种叫肌萎缩侧索硬化的病。活动要求参与者在网络上发布自己被冰水浇遍全身的视频内容，然后该参与者邀请至少三人来参与这一活动。被邀请者要么在 24 小时内接受挑战,要么选择为"肌萎缩侧索硬化病"ALS 协会至少捐赠 100 美元,或两者都做。

Raised by a group of ALS organizations in the United States, ice bucket challenge is an activity that tend to draw public's attention to motor neuron disease. The challenge encourages nominated participants to be filmed having a bucket of ice water poured on their heads and then nominating at least three persons to do the same. A common stipulation is that nominated participants have 24 hours to comply or a minimum 100 US dollar donation to the ALS organizations is required or participants can engage in both options.

活动体验馆　Activity Experience Pavilion

金金和湾湾在日常生活中收集了一些公益广告图片和宣传语。让我们来分享吧！

Jinjin and Wanwan collected some public welfare advertisements pictures and slogans in daily life. Let us share them.

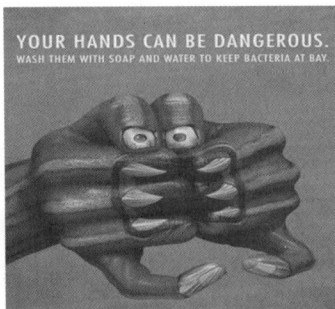

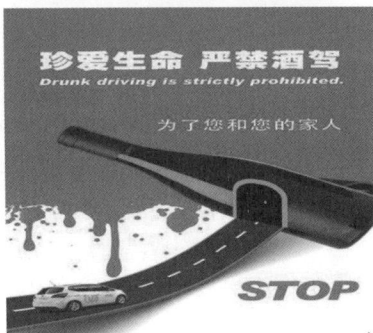

欣赏完以上的公益广告图片和宣传语,请同学们写出以下这些公益广告的英文。

After enjoying the public welfare advertisement pictures and slogans, please write down the following public welfare advertisement in English.

你能不能也设计出让大家印象深刻的广告宣传图? 试一试!

Can you design an impressive advertisement picture? Have a try!

第三节　环境保护

Section 3　Environmental Protection

身边小事　Little Things around Us

金金:前几天下了一场台风雨,我家小区门口的路被淹了,积水深度达到1米。小区外面停着的车被淹了,我们小区的住户无法正常出入,你看多可怕!我们的环境好像越来越差了。

湾湾:这有两方面原因:一方面大雨刚好碰到了大海涨潮,我们沿海地区地势较低,只比海平面略高,涨潮的时候基本与海平面持平,因此积水无法快速排入大海;另一方面则是排水渠堵塞,排水不畅,这是人为因素造成的。

Jinjin: A few days ago under a gust of typhoon rain, my neighborhood door of the road was flooded. Water depth reached a meter. The cars were also flooded. Our community residents could not go in or out. How terrible! Our environment seems to be getting worse.

Wanwan: There are two reasons. On the one hand, the heavy rain just met the tide of the sea, and our coastal areas are lower, only slightly higher than the sea level. So in the high tide when the sea level is higher, stagnant water can not be quickly discharged into the sea. On the other hand, drains are clogged and drainage is not smooth, which is caused by human factors.

大家共言 Common Topic

我们不注重保护环境,一味地对自然环境进行肆意破坏,而不懂得保护和合理利用,就会导致更多的自然灾害的发生,最终受伤害的还是我们。就比如一场台风雨就让我们遭受到巨大的经济损失,甚至威胁到我们的人身安全。

We do not pay attention to protecting the environment, harming the natural environment and do not know how to protect it for reasonable use. It will lead to more natural disasters, and ultimately hurt us. For example, a typhoon caused huge economic losses, and even threaten personal safety.

幸运的是,现在越来越多的人认识到环境保护的重要性,对我们赖以生存的地球给予了更多的关注和保护,认识到对水、土地等其他自然资源进行合理的开发、使用的重要性。

Fortunately, nowadays more and more people realize the importance of environmental protection, give more attention and protection to the earth we depend on, and realize the importance of rational development and use of other natural resources such as water and land.

少年观天下 Youth's View of the World

地球是我们共同的美好家园,世界各国都在重视保护环境,国际环保组织商定了一系列的环境保护日,呼吁更多的人保护环境、爱护我们的家园。下面是一些相关的环境保护日,你知道几个呢?

Earth is our common home, all countries are attaching importance to the protection of the environment. International environmental organizations agreed on a series of environmental protection days and call for more people to pay attention to environmental protection and love our homes. Here are some relevant days of environmental protection. How many environment protection days do you know?

3 月 21 日:国际森林日

March 21st : International Day of Forests

3 月 22 日:世界水日

March 22nd : World Water Day

3 月 23 日:世界气象日

March 23rd : World Meteorological Day

4 月 22 日:世界地球日

April 22nd : World Earth Day

　　我们国家还根据我们的国情,确立了植树节和全国土地日,倡导大家植树造林,优化环境,合理利用土地资源,保护地球。

　　On account of the condition of our country, Tree Planting Day and National Land Day were set up to advocate afforestation, environment improvement, land resource utilization and earth protection.

3 月 12 日:中国植树节

March 12th : Tree Planting Day of China

6 月 25 日:全国土地日

June 25th : China Land Day

6 月 5 日：世界环境日
June 5th：World Environment Day

6 月 17 日：世界防治荒漠化和干旱日
June 17th：World Day to Combat Desertification

活动体验馆 Activity Experience Pavilion

我们应该从身边的小事做起，爱护地球，保护我们共同的家园。和你的朋友或家人讨论一下，让我们从以下几方面开始实施行动吧！

We should take care of the earth and protect our common home from the small things around us. Discuss it with your friends or family. Let's start with the following steps.

自然资源 Natural Resources	怎么做? How to do ?
水 Water	
空气 Air	
土地 Land	
保护动、植物 Protect Animals and Plants	
垃圾处理 Garbage disposal	

第四节　和谐平等

Section 4　Harmony and Equality

📖 身边小事　**Little Things around Us**

　　今年暑假,金金和湾湾来到英国进行为期 20 天的游学之旅,他们与寄宿家庭一起生活。第一天午餐的时候,寄宿家庭的爸爸妈妈准备了三明治和沙拉。金金感觉吃不饱,心里嘀咕老外"抠",可由于不好意思而又不主动交流,更不敢去索要。同学们,如果你是金金,你会怎么做呢?

　　This summer holiday, Jinjin and Wanwan went on a study tour in Britain for 20 days. They lived with the home-stay family. The first lunch in Britain, father and mother in home-stay family prepared sandwiches and salad. Jinjin thought the food was not enough and thought the home-stay family was mean to them. And Jinjin was too shy to ask for more food to eat. My dear classmates, what will you do if you are Jinjin?

📖 大家共言　**Common Topic**

　　生活在不同文化背景下的人,会有不同的待人处事方式。由于文化的差异,来自不同国家的人在交往时便可能会产生一些误会。让我们一起来看几则因为文化差异而产生的小误会。

　　People from different cultures have different ways to get along with others. Misunderstanding might happen between people from different countries because of the cultural differences. Let's take a look at several examples of small misunderstandings which are because of the culture difference.

　　情景一:当别人称赞你的新裙子真漂亮时,你一般会怎么回答? 如果你回答的是"哪里哪里……"

　　Scene One: When someone compliments on your new dress, what will you say? If your answer is "It's so so (Where)..."

这个人怎么这么有意思，我已经告诉她裙子很漂亮，她还问我哪里漂亮，那就告诉她"裙子"。

Oh, what a funny girl she is. I've told her that the dress was beautiful. She even asks me to point out where she looks beautiful. I might answer "Your dresss".

情景二: 你的西班牙朋友邀你一起吃饭,饭后他却说要和你平分账单,你会怎么想?

Scene Two: Your Spanish friend invites you for a dinner together. After that he advises you to share the bill, what will you think?

这是理所当然的，在我们国家，即使是最好的朋友在一起吃饭，也是AA制。

It is very common in our country. We share the bill of dinner even among the best friends.

情景三: 当你在马来西亚朋友家吃饭,你的朋友递给你食物时,你能用左手接过食物吗?

Scene Three: When your Malaysian friend invites you to have a dinner at home, your friend brings you food, can you take the food with your left hand?

当你与马来西亚人握手或拿食物时要用右手，我们认为左手是不洁净的。

When you shake hands or take food from Malaysian, please use your right hand. Left hand is considered unclean.

情景四：你认识一位英国朋友，问他："你几岁了?"或"你一个月赚多少钱?"你觉得英国朋友会做什么反应?

Scene Four: When you meet with a British friend and ask him "How old are you? "or "How much money do you earn every month?" Do you think what reaction will he have on your questions?

> 这是我的隐私，为什么要告诉你呢? 跟我谈论天气吧。

This is my private information. Why should I tell you? Let's talk about the weather.

（本节资料摘录自 Never Do These Things in Foreign Countries。想要获取更多资料，请观看 https://v.youku.com/v_show/id_XMzc5NDU3NDI2OA==.html）

少年观天下　Youth's View of the World

澳大利亚和谐日

澳大利亚是典型的移民国家，被社会学家喻为"民族的拼盘"。自欧洲移民踏上这片美丽的土地之日起，已先后有来自世界 120 个国家、140 个民族的移民到澳大利亚谋生和发展。

每年的 3 月 21 日，澳大利亚举国上下以丰富多彩的形式庆祝"和谐日"的到来。和谐日始于 1999 年，恰逢联合国消除种族歧视国际日。每年人们都会聚在一起参加当地的活动。和谐日一直传播"人人归属"的理念，旨在提高人们对不同文化的认识、接纳与包容以消除歧视。

该活动已经成为澳大利亚最重要的多元文化的盛事。它关乎包容、尊重以及人的归属感。

Harmony Day in Australia

Australia is a typical immigrant country which is regarded as "ethnic platter" by sociologists. Since the Permanent European have arrived in the beautiful land, more than 120 countries and 140 ethical immigrations have settled in Australia.

Harmony Day is celebrated by colorful forms annually on March 21st in Australia. Harmony Day began in 1999, coinciding with the United Nations International Day for the Elimination of Racial Discrimination. Each year, it is marked by people coming together and participating in local activities. The continuing message of Harmony Day is "Everyone Belongs". It aims to raise awareness, acceptance and inclusion of different cultures and to eliminate discrimination.

Harmony Day celebrates Australia's cultural diversity. It's about inclusiveness, respect and a sense of belonging for everyone.

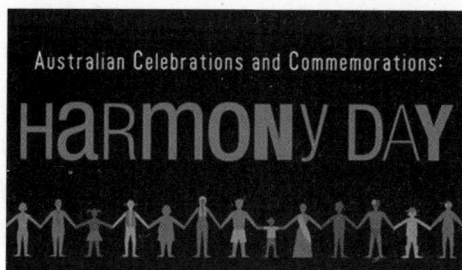

如何庆祝和谐日？

How to Celebrate the Harmony Day?

:每年和谐日,社区会举办各种各样的庆祝活动。这是一个庆祝彼此传统并分享故事的日子。

Each year in Harmony Day, celebration events are held in every community. It's a day to celebrate each other's traditions and share stories.

:和谐日的官方颜色是橙色。它代表着人们之间的沟通与有效交谈。因此,我们会穿橙色的衣服或者佩戴橙色的物件。

The official color of Harmony Day is Orange. It represents the communications and meaningful conversations between people. So we will dress something in orange on that day.

:和谐日当天,我们会带上家乡的食物并与同学分享。

On Harmony Day, we will come to school with the ethnic foods to share with our classmates.

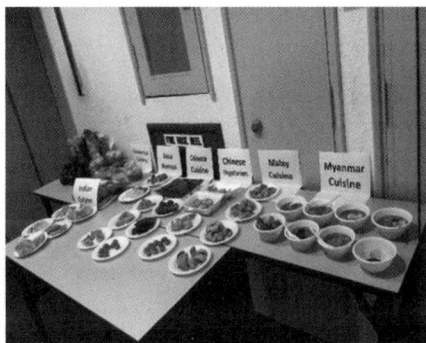

:对待文化差异,不应该排斥,而应该沟通。既要继承发扬中国传统文化精华,又要尊重学习其他民族文化的价值,主张平等交流、相互学习。

Sufficient communication, instead of repulsion, should be adopted in the face of the culture difference. We should inherit and carry forward the essence of Chinese traditional culture, and fully respect other cultures. Advocate a mutual studying and exchange culture on a equal basis.

活动体验馆　Activity Experience Pavilion

活动 1:亲爱的同学们,你们看过《舌尖上的中国》这部纪录片吗? 它在播出过程中获得了很高的收视率。为什么我们喜欢这部关于食物的电视节目呢? 因为每个人都喜爱美味的食物,而且它是联系人与人之间的有效途径。当你们第一次见面时,你会发现彼此的不同,但是一旦你们坐下来吃饭的时候,你会留意存在于食物和文化之中的相似之处。尽管你们会因为所吃食物的不同而感到别扭,从长远来看,这是不同的食物让你特别。那么你能为班里的同学烹煮一道你家乡的美食并在班级分享吗？请写下你的食谱，或者拍摄成视频并上传至视频分享网站。

Activity 1: Dear classmates, have you ever watched the Documentary *A Bite of China*? It attracted high ratings during its airing. Why do we love this food show? Because everyone loves delicious food, and it's a great way for people to connect. It's very easy when you first meet a person to notice their differences but when you sit down and eat together, you'll notice similarities in both food and culture. Even though you might feel awkward by eating something different, in the long run that's what's going to make you special. So can you cook your hometown food and share in class? Please write down your recipe or make videos and upload them to a sharing video site.

热干面

Hot Dry Noodles

饺子

Jiaozi/Dumplings

麻婆豆腐

Mapo Tofu

春卷

Spring Rolls

活动2：制作馅饼

同学们，请根据以下菜谱或者网上的视频，动手制作馅饼。

Activity 2：Making pancakes

Boys and girls，try to make pancakes with the following recipe or video.

第四章　大湾区变化
Chapter 4　The Change of Great Bay Area

　　粤港澳大湾区是指由香港、澳门两个特别行政区和广东省的广州、深圳、珠海、佛山、中山、东莞、肇庆、江门、惠州等九市组成的城市群,是与美国纽约湾区、旧金山湾区和日本东京湾区比肩的世界四大湾区之一。粤港澳大湾区面积达5.6万平方千米,人口达6 600万。2017年GDP(国内生产总值)突破10万亿元,湾区GDP总量规模超过俄罗斯,在世界国家排行中名列第11位,成为全国经济最活跃的地区之一。

　　Guangdong-Hong Kong-Macao Greater Bay Area consists of both Hong Kong and Macao SARs and Guangzhou, Shenzhen, Zhuhai, Foshan, Zhongshan, Dongguan, Zhaoqing, Jiangmen, Huizhou nine cities. It is one of the world's four great bay areas, the other great lay areas are the United States New York Bay area, the San Francisco Bay area and Japan Tokyo bay area. The area is 56, 000 square kilometers with a population of 66 million. Its GDP in 2017 reached 10 trillion Yuan, ranking 11th in the world, surpassing Russia, becoming one of the most active areas in the national economy.

第一节 幸福大湾区

Section 1   The Great Bay Area of Happiness

身边小事 Little Things around Us

暑假到来了,金金回了趟老家,一周后再次回到金湾的家,变得更加勤奋起来。每天按计划去学习、生活。"妈妈,我去跑步了。"早上金金跟妈妈说。他住的小区既大又美,他在这跑步的时候可以享受新鲜的空气。跑步回来开始学习直到中午。

然后他接到湾湾打来的电话:"金金,我们同学下午想去图书馆,你要跟我们一起去吗?""好主意! 我正想问你几道数学问题。"金金回答。图书馆是新的,又舒服又安静,是一个学习的好地方。

晚饭后,金金的父母亲带他和他的妹妹到海边散步! 看! 他们是多么幸福啊!

Summer holiday is coming. Jinjin goes back to hometown. After a week he comes back to Jinwan. He studies harder than before. Study and live as planned every day. "Mum, I am going to run." He says to his mother in the morning. He lives in the neighborhood that is so big and beautiful. When he runs here he can enjoy the fresh air. Then he begins to study after running till noon.

Then Wanwan calls him: "Jinjin, our classmates want to the library this afternoon. Would you like to go with us?" "Good idea. Then I can ask you some math questions." Jinjin answers. The library is new, comfortable and quiet. It's a good place to study.

After dinner, Jinjin's parents take him and his young sister to walk on the seaside. Look! How happy they are!

优美的环境
Beautiful Environment

金海岸文化艺术中心
Jinhaian Culture Art Center

在图书馆读书
Read in the Library

在海边漫步
Walk on the Seaside

大家共言　Comment Topic

一天,我们有幸观看了历史老师刘昌言制作的历史片。

刘老师问:"你们知道关于三灶的历史吗?"

一位学生回答:"是的。当三灶被日本侵略时,有300多人被活埋。很惨!"

另一位学生说:"过去人们吃不饱,他们总是挨饿。"

又一位学生说:"他们不能上学,他们很穷。"

"是的。那你们现在幸福吗? 为什么呢?"刘老师又问。

"当然。我感觉很幸福。我们不仅有衣服穿,还穿得美。我们不仅有住的地方,还住得舒服。我们不仅能吃得饱,而且总能吃上美食,如海鲜。"一位学生说。

然后班长举手,老师让他来回答:"和平是他们用生命换来的,三灶发展得越来越好,交通发达,生活便捷。所以我们一定要好好学习,回报祖国,不让历史重演。"

One day, we had a chance to watch a video which was made by a history teacher Liu Changyan.

Mr. Liu asked: "Do you know the history about Sanzao?"

One student answered: "Yes. When Sanzao was invaded by Japanese, there were more than 300 people buried alive. So terrible!"

Another student said: "The people couldn't have enough to eat in the past. They were always hungry."

Another student said: "The children had no chance to go to school. They were poor."

"Yeah. And are you happy now? Why?" Mr. Liu asked again.

"Of course. I feel very happy. Not only do we have clothes to wear, but also we have beautiful ones. Not only do we have shelters, but we live comfortably. We can not only eat enough, but also eat delicious food, such as sea food." One student said.

And the monitor put up his hand and the teacher let him answer: "Peace is what they have brought with their lives. Sanzao develops better and better. Transportation is developed and life is convenient. We must study hard to repay our motherland. Let history not repeat itself."

三灶万人坟

Ten Thousand People Grave in Sanzao

讲述三灶的故事

Telling the History about Sanzao

海鲜　Sea Food

购物中心　Shopping Mall

少年观天下　Youth's View of the World

大湾区之海
——港珠澳大桥

　　港珠澳大桥是连接香港、珠海、澳门的超大型跨海通道,全长 55 千米,其中主体工程"海中桥隧"长 29.6 千米,海底隧道长 6.75 千米,是世界最长的跨海大桥。同时,港珠澳大桥是国家高速公路网中 G4——京港澳高速与 G94——珠三角环线高速的部分路段。

　　港珠澳大桥沉管隧道是全球最长的公路沉管隧道和全球唯一的深埋沉管隧道,生产和安装技术有一系列创新,为世界海底隧道工程技术提供了独特的样本和宝贵的经验。

The Sea of the Greater Bay Area
—Hong Kong-Zhuhai-Macao Bridge

Hong Kong-Zhuhai-Macao Bridge is the super-large cross-sea passage linking Hong Kong, Zhuhai and Macao. It is 55 kilometers long. One of the main projects "bridge tunnel under the sea" is 29.6 km long. The tunnel is about 6.75 kilometers long. It becomes the world's longest cross-sea bridge. At the same time, the Hong Kong-Zhuhai-Macao bridge is part of the G4—Beijing-Hong Kong-Macao expressway and G94—Pearl River delta ring line expressway in the national highway network.

The Hong Kong-Zhuhai-Macao bridge immersed tube tunnel is the world's longest highway immersed tube tunnel and the world's only deep buried tube tunnel. There are a number of innovations in its production and installation techniques. It provides unique samples and valuable experience for the world undersea tunnel engineering technology.

港珠澳大桥

Hong Kong–Zhuhai–Macao Bridge

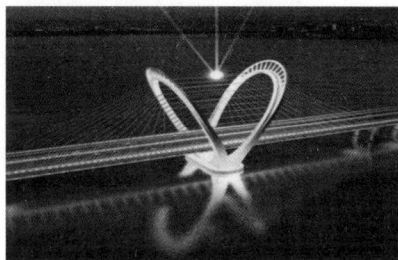

金海大桥

Jinhai Bridge

大湾区之空

中国国际航空航天博览会简称中国(珠海)航展或珠海航展,是国际性专业航空航天展览,以实物展示、贸易洽谈、学术交流和飞行表演为主要特征的国际性专业航空航天展览会。

1996 年成功举办首届航展,然后每两年举办一次。现已发展成为集贸易性、专业性、观赏性为一体的,代表当今国际航空航天业先进科技主流,展示当今世界航空航天业发展水平的盛会,是世界五大最具国际影响力的航展之一。

The Sky of the Great Bay Area

China International Air and Space Expo is referred to as China (Zhuhai) Airshow or Zhuhai Airshow. It is an international professional aerospace exhibition. International professional aviation and aerospace exhibition features material display, trade negotiation, academic exchange and flight performance.

The first airshow was successfully held in 1996. And then it is held every two years. It has developed into an activity of trade, profession, appreciation. It represents today's the advanced technology of international aerospace industry and the development level of the aerospace industry in the world. It is one of the world's five most influential airshows.

身在珠海金湾,这是让人感到多么兴奋、骄傲和自豪的事情! 厉害了! 我的大湾区!

We live here, we are proud of it! How great the Bay will be!

活动体验馆 Activity Experience Pavilion

习近平主席说"绿水青山就是金山银山"。所以我们必须保护空气、海水、海洋生物,珍爱我们所拥有的一切,让我们永远幸福生活下去! 根据以下信息,你能完成后面的表格吗?

Chinese President Xi Jinping says: "Beautiful environment is worth gold and silver." So we must protect the air, the water of the sea and sea animals. We should cherish what we have. Let's be happy forever! Can you finish the following form according to the information below?

※Humans catch whales for meat, fat and oil

※Eat small fish and other sea life

※Jumping high out of the water

※Rules on whale protection

※Huge

※Water pollution

※Live in the sea

※Some have teeth

※Learn more about whales

※Stop throwing rubbish in the sea

※Sing songs

※Whale parts sold to make things like candles and soap

它们是什么样子的？ What do they look like?	
它们住在哪里？ Where do they live?	
它们吃什么？ What do they eat?	
它们能做什么？ What can they do?	
它们之中有些为什么必须受到保护？ Why do some of them have to be protected?	
我们如何保护它们？ How can we protect them?	

第二节 腾飞教育
Section 2　Soaring Education

身边小事　Little Things around Us

金金:哇,这个学校好热闹啊! 我们一起去瞧一瞧吧!

湾湾:看! 同学们都面向鲜艳的团旗,举起右手大声宣誓。今天是什么日子?

金金:哦,我知道了! 今天是五四青年节。他们是在参加入团仪式呢!

Jinjin: Wow! Here is a school with energy and liveliness. Let's go and see!

Wanwan: look! Facing the red flag of Communist Youth League, all of the students are raising their right hands to take an oath. What's special about today?

Jinjin: I see! Today is May 4th. It is Youth Day today. They are participating in the ceremony of joining the Communist Youth League.

入团仪式

The Ceremony of Joining the Communist Youth League

湾湾:听! 同学们在唱歌呢! 唱得真好听!

金金:他们唱的是中国共青团团歌《光荣啊,中国共青团》。多么好听的歌曲啊!

湾湾:瞧! 新团员带上了团徽!

金金:恭喜他们成为一名中国共青团团员!

Wanwan: Listen! The students are singing! Sounds great!

Jinjin: They are singing the song of Chinese Communist Youth League, that is *Glorious, Communist Youth League of China*. What a beautiful song!

Wanwan: Look! The new League members are wearing the League badge.

Jinjin: Congratulations!

大家共言　Common Topic

在五四青年节这天,金金和湾湾亲眼见证了金湾区四所公办中学的入团仪式。现在让我们一起去参观大湾区的这些学校吧!

On May 4th, Jinjin and Wanwan witnessed the ceremony of joining the Communist Youth League in Jinwan District. Now it's time to visit the public middle schools with them!

♥红旗中学 Hongqi Junior High School

珠海市红旗中学始办于 1971 年(原名珠海市红旗一中),至今已有 50 多年的办学历史,它位于红旗镇,校园占地面积近 5 000 平方米。学校分为教学区、运动区、生活区三个相对独立的区域,三区互不干扰。

Founded in 1971, known as Hongqi No. 1 Middle School, Hongqi Junior High School has a history of more than 50 years. Located in Hongqi Town, Hongqi Junior High School covers the area of 5,000 square meters. The school consists of teaching area, sports area and living area, which are separate from each other.

红旗中学大门

The Gate of Hongqi Junior High School

歌咏活动

The Chorus Competition

♥小林中学 Xiaolin Junior High School

小林中学成立于 1964 年,坐落在红旗镇钟灵毓秀的小林山下。目前校园占地面积 30 577.5 平方米,现代教学设施一应俱全。校内主要建筑有教学楼、办公楼、实验楼和学生宿舍楼。校园景色优美,绿树成荫。

Founded in 1964, Xiaolin Junior High School is situated in the beautiful Xiaolin mountain of Hongqi Town. Now covering the area of 30, 577. 5 square meters, its campus is equipped with advanced multimedia classrooms, office area, laboratories and students' dormitory buildings. Xiaolin Junior High School is beautiful and shade by trees.

小林中学校门

The Gate of Xiaolin Junior High School

教室

the Classroom

♥金海岸中学 Jinhaian Junior High School

金海岸中学是该区唯一所同时获评省一级学校和市级绿色学校的完全中

学。金海岸中学创建于 1992 年 9 月,坐落在三灶镇,校园占地面积 40 000 平方米。作为全国航空特色示范学校之一的金海岸中学,在全国青少年航天科普大赛中屡获佳绩。

Jinhaian Junior High School is not only one of the provincial first-rate junior high school, but also is one of the municipal green middle school. Founded in September 1992, it is located in Sanzao Town with an area of 40,000 square meters. As one of the national school featuring aviation training and education, it has made remarkable achievements in YASC (Youth Aerospace Science Competition).

金海岸中学周边环境

The Surroundings of Jinhaian Junior High School

学校音乐会

The School Concert

♥三灶中学 Sanzao Junior High School

作为金湾区第一所省一级中学,三灶中学创建于 1957 年,地处有深厚人文底蕴的三灶岛, 学校占地面积 34 321 平方米。它是一所以体育艺术为特色项目的学校,同时,体育竞赛水平一直保持在珠海市的前列。

As the first provincial first-rate junior high school, Sanzao Junior High School was founded in 1957. Located in Sanzao Island, Sanzao Junior High School covers an area of 34,321 square meters. Sanzao Junior High School is famous with its sports and art featuring education. Meanwhile, its successful achievements keep ahead in Zhuhai.

体育课

P. E. Lesson

艺术团

The Art Department

少年观天下 Youth's View of the World

游览了金湾区的四所公办中学后,金金、湾湾带大家再去其他国家看一看,了解一下国外的中学教育有什么特点。

After visiting four public junior high schools, Jinjin and Wanwan are supposed to travel around the world to know more about secondary education in other countries.

♥ 美国 the USA

美国的中学生于早上八点四十五分上课,中午十二点在学校吃午餐。在午餐后,他们会睡一会儿。下午一点半开始上课,三点四十五分放学。美国的学生每天上六节课,一周上五天。

In junior high school in America, pupils start with their classes at 8:45 a.m.. At 12 o'clock, the students eat lunch at school. After lunch, students have a nap for a short time. They begin classes at 1:30 p.m. in the afternoon and end the class at 3:45 p.m.. They go to school on weekdays and have 6 classes every day.

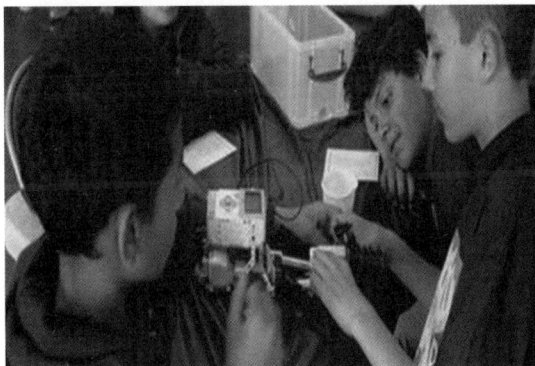

信息技术课
Information Technology Class

写作课

Writing Class

♥英国 the UK

在英国,小朋友在 11 岁小学毕业以后,就可以升入中学了。其实英国的中学并没有那么明确的标明初中高中,他们的初中一般指的是七年级到十一年级这五年。中学包括 9~12 年级或初中 6 或 7 到 9 年级,高中 10~12 年级。关于英国学生的学校生活,一般的学校都是从早晨九点上课,下午四点放学。四点过后,学生大多去参加各种各样的课外活动。

Graduating from primary school at the age of 11, students in the UK become a high school students. Secondary schools are also called high schools in the UK, covering grades 9-12, the junior high school 6 or 7-9 and the high school 10-12. The students have classes from 9: 00 a. m. to 4: 00 p. m. . After school, most of the students participates in different kinds of activities.

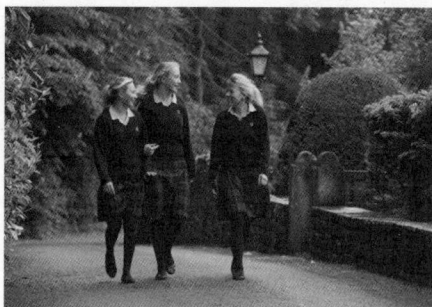

校园里讨论的学生

Students Discussing in School

阅读课 Reading Class

♥德国 Germany

德国中学生根据其成绩可以从四种形式中供选择学校,分别是职业预科、实科中学、文理中学和综合学校。成绩较好的学生通常到文理中学就读,文理中学学制通常为 8~9 年;成绩次好的学生常常会进入实科中学,学制为 5~6 年;成绩再次的学生则就读 5 年制的职业预科;而综合学校是上述三种传统学校类型的组合,通常包括 5 或 7~10 年级。德国的初中生通常都是早七点左右上课,下午一点半点左右结束当天的课程,在课程结束后才能午休。

In Germany, after children complete their primary education, there are four options for secondary schooling: Gymnasium (grammar school), Realschule, Mittelschule and Gesamtschule sorted by the quality and relevance of the exit exam. Students with better grades usually go to a liberal arts secondary school, which usually lasts for 8-9 years. Students with the next best grades usually go to a real secondary school, which lasts for 5-6 years. Students who repeat are enrolled in a 5-year pre-vocational school, while comprehensive schools are a combination of the three traditional school types mentioned above and usually include grades 5 or 7-10. Junior high school students in Germany usually start classes around 7: 00 a. m. and finish the day's classes around 1: 30 p. m. , with a lunch break at the end of the course.

体育课 **P. E. Class**

踢足球 **Playing Soccer**

♥日本 Japan

在日本,中学生通常都是早八点四十五分上课,上午上四节课,每节课50分钟。下午上课的时间是从一点四十五分到三点三十分。课后大部分学生都参加学校社团活动,每天大约两个小时。

In Japan, the school begins at 8: 45 am. and there are four 50-minute classes. Pupils have afternoon classes from 1: 45 to 3: 35 p. m.. Many students participate in after-school clubs, which lasts for two hours every day.

上课中 **Having Class**

剑道部 **Kendo Department**

活动体验馆 Activity Experience Pavilion

放学后,同学们的课后活动都不一样。请你调查一下不同国家或地区的学生的课后活动内容,并讨论相同点和不同点。

After school, students are participating in different and colorful activities. Now please do a survey about after school activities in different countries or areas, and talk about them.

国家/地区 Country/Areas	相同点 Similarity	不同点 Differences
中国香港 Hong Kong, China		
中国澳门 Macao, China		
中国其他省份 Other provinces in China		
美国 the United States		
英国 The UK		
德国 Germany		
日本 Japan		

第三节 珠海新貌
Section 3　A New Look of Zhuhai

身边小事　Little Things around Us

　　暑假来临了,金金和湾湾打算到珠海海滨公园玩。经过珠海大剧院时,他们被两个漂亮的大"贝壳"建筑深深吸引住了。

　　Summer vacation is coming. Jinjin and Wanwan are going to play in the Zhuhai Seaside Park. When they pass the Zhuhai Opera House, they are deeply attracted by two beautiful "shell" buildings.

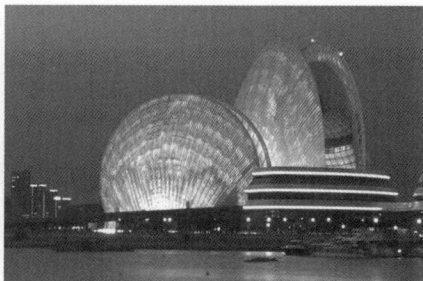

珠海大剧院　**Zhuhai Opera House**

　　金金:这两个漂亮的大"贝壳"就是珠海大剧院,它位于情侣路野狸岛海滨,是中国唯一建设在海岛上的歌剧院。它就像是一大一小两组"贝壳"的形体,白天呈现半通透效果,一到夜晚则像月光一样晶莹剔透,所以又名"日月贝"。

　　JinJin: The two beautiful "shells" are Zhuhai Opera House, which is located on the beach of Beaver Island of lover Road, the only opera house built on the island in China. It is like a large and small group of "shells". It shows a half-transparent effect during the day, and at night it is like the crystal clear moon, so it is also called "sun and moon shells".

　　珠海大剧院采用世界先进声、光学设计和舞台工艺设计。大剧场可容纳1 600人,由前厅、观众厅和舞台三部分组成,满足大型歌舞剧、音乐剧、芭蕾舞剧、话剧、交响乐、大型综合演出等需要。小剧场可容纳 500 人。

The Zhuhai Opera House uses the world's advanced sound, optical design and stage craft design. The Grand Theater can accommodate 1,600 people, consisting of a front hall, an auditorium and a stage. It meets the needs of large-scale operas, musicals, ballets, plays, symphonies and large-scale comprehensive performances. The small theater can accommodate 500 people.

湾湾:珠海变得越来越漂亮了,就在 2017 年珠海还诞生了首个国家级地标建筑,珠澳第一高楼——珠海中心大厦。

Wanwan: Zhuhai is becoming more and more beautiful. In 2017, the first national landmark building Zhuhai Tower, the tallest building in Zhuhai and Macao was born.

珠海中心大厦 **Zhuhai Tower**

大家共言 Common Topic

小朋友们都在热烈讨论着:

Children are discussing heatedly:

A:世界最长的跨海大桥——港珠澳大桥已落成! 从此我们去港珠澳更快、更便捷! 珠海将成为全国唯一一个与港澳陆桥相连的城市。

A: The world's longest cross sea bridge, the Hong Kong-Zhuhai-Macao Bridge has been completed. From now on, we can go to Hong Kong, Zhuhai and Macao faster and more conveniently. Zhuhai will become the only city in the country that is connected to Hong Kong and Macao by bridge.

B:珠海机场有望升级为国际机场。未来珠海机场保障能力将提升至 1 200

万人次,航班会越来越多,珠海人坐飞机出行将越来越方便。

B: Zhuhai Airport is expected to be upgraded to an international airport. In the future, the capacity of Zhuhai Airport will be upgraded to 12 million passengers. Flights will increase in number and frequency. It will be more and more convenient for Zhuhai people to travel by air.

港珠澳大桥

Hong Kong–Zhuhai–Macao Bridge

珠海机场

Zhuhai Airport

C:珠海公交迎来大变革! 刷手机乘公交,微信、支付宝直接扫码上车, 再也不用担心忘记带零钱了!

C: Zhuhai public transport is facing great changes. Use the phone to pay: scan the QR code in WeChat, Alipay and you no longer need to worry about forgetting to take the change!

D:教育大变样。2018 年,珠海人迎来众多新校园的使用和开工,如金湾一中和金湾区航空新城小学。

D: Education has changed dramatically. In 2018, Zhuhai people will usher in the construction and use of many new campuses, such as Jinwan No. 1 High School and Jinwan Aviation New Town Primary School.

扫码

Scanning Code

E:产业更发达。横琴长隆第二主题公园继现有的长隆一期后,还将投资超500亿,建横琴长隆第二主题公园,包括全世界独一无二,且规模最大的海洋博物馆。世界三大主题公园品牌之一的乐高主题乐园将落户珠海,这将是中国南部第一家乐高主题公园。

E: More developed industry—The second Hengqin Chimelong theme park will absorb an investment of more than 50 billion yuan, including the world's unique and largest marine museum. Lego theme park, one of the world's three major theme park brands, will be built in Zhuhai, which will be the first Lego theme park in South China.

长隆海洋王国

Chimelong Ocean Kingdom

金金:在城市的建筑或设计上珠海一直走在全国的前沿,还有一大波新颖的城市。建筑将如巨人般在珠海拔地而起,说不定哪天就成为国家下一个新地标了!

Jinjin: Zhuhai has always been at the forefront of the nation in urban architecture or design, and a large wave of new urban buildings will rise like giants in Zhuhai. Maybe one day it will be the next national landmark!

少年观天下　Youth's View of the World

金金:珠海是一座充满期待和惊喜的城市。现在的珠海正在发生日新月异的变化。你看!

Jinjin: Zhuhai is a city full of expectations and surprises. Now Zhuhai is changing with each passing day. Look!

景点越来越多

More Scenic Spots

交通越来越方便

More Convenient Traffic

道路越来越整洁

Cleaner and Tidier Roads

绿道越来越多

More Green Ways

住房小区越来越美

More Beautiful Communities

活动体验馆 Activity Experience Pavilion

亲爱的同学们,我们通过以上的图文了解了珠海近年来的一些变化,你还能说出珠海更多的变化吗?你可以通过调查访问、观察、查资料等方式得到你的新发现,请将它们记录下来。

My dear classes, we have known some changes of Zhuhai in recent years. Can you tell us more? You can get your new findings through investigation and interview, observation and information searching. Please write them down.

珠海的变化

The Great Changes in Zhuhai

	以前 before	现在 Now
道路 Road		
交通工具 Transportation		
建筑物 Building		

第四节 金湾巨变
Section 4 The Great Changes of Jinwan

身边小事 Little Things around Us

当你来到珠海市金湾区,你就可以看到你身边身着红色马甲的志愿者。他们也许在指挥行人过马路,也许在路边或者山上捡垃圾,也许在公共场所帮人指路,也许在护送孩子上下学,也许在帮助老师们组织"六一"儿童节活动,等等。随着金湾区经济的飞速发展,人们的文明素养也在飞速提升。人们以参加志愿者、服务社会为荣,不分年龄、性别、种族。他们的无私奉献精神在金湾区已经遍地开花。大学生走进校园,走进小学生的课堂,为他们上了一节又一节生动活泼的活动课。心理教育咨询师走进家庭,为各个家庭排忧解难。有些年龄大的老人不顾严寒酷热,为了避免不必要的交通事故,他们依然放弃自己的休息时间,走上了马路。这一个个鲜红的红马甲,走在金湾的大地上,成为一道亮丽的风景线。

When you come to Jinwan District of Zhuhai City, you can see volunteers in red vests by your side. They may be directing pedestrians to cross the road, perhaps picking up rubbish on the roadside or on the mountain, perhaps guiding people in public places, perhaps escorting children to and from school. They may also help teachers organize June 1 International Children's Day activities, and so on. With the rapid development of Jinwan economy, people's literacy is also developing rapidly. People are honored to volunteer, serve the society, regardless of age, gender, race. Their selfless dedication can be seen everywhere in Jinwan District. College students come into the schoolyard, go into the classroom of pupils, and take one lively activity lessons for them. Psychological education counselors come into the family to solve the difficulties for each family. Some older people, despite cold or heat, gave up their rest time and served on the road in order to reduce traffic accidents. The red vests, walking on the ground of the Jinwan District, make a beautiful view.

指挥行人过马路

Directing Pedestrians to Cross the Road

清理垃圾

Cleaning up Rubbish

义务咨询

Giving Advice for Free

大家共言　Common Topic

　　随着经济的发展,人们越来越重视对孩子的教育投资,也越来越注重生活的品质。这也是社会发展和进步的必然趋势。这两年,金湾区为了顺应时代的发展,引入高科技人才,不惜重金投资、新建了广东省实验中学金湾分校、航空新城小学、航空新城幼儿园。一座座美丽的校园拔地而起,它们是发展和进步的希望。

　　便利的交通是经济发展的纽带。为了更好地赶上市区发展的步伐,金湾区建立了金湾立交桥。它就像一条条蟒蛇交错缠绕,宏伟而壮观,为人们的工作和生活提供了更加便利的交通环境。

With the development of economy, people pay more and more attention to their children's education investment and quality of life. This is also the inevitable trend of social development and progress. In the past two years, in order to adapt to the development of the times and the introduction of high technology talents, Jinwan District has invested heavily in the construction of Jinwan Branch of Guangdong Experimental Middle School, Aviation Newtown Primary School and Aviation Newtown Kindergarten. One by one beautiful campuses rise as the hope of development and progress.

Convenient transportation is the link of economic development. In order to better keep up with the pace with the urban area development, Jinwan has built the Jinwan Overpass. It looks like a python intertwining, magnificent and spectacular. It provides more convenient transportation for people's work and life.

广东省实验中学金湾分校

Jinwan Branch of Guangdong Experimental Middle School

金湾立交桥

Jinwan Overpass

航空新城幼儿园

Aviation Newtown Kindergarten

航空新城小学

Aviation Newtown Primary School

少年观天下　Youth's View of the World

"少年强,则国强;少年进步,则国进步"。当今的世界是科技的世界。为了培养国家科技人才,金湾区注重从娃娃抓起。从2016年6月,金湾区为金湾一小、三板小学、小林实验小学、三灶中心小学、海澄小学等5所学校建立了不同主题的创客空间(金湾一小"多元跨学科综合校园创客空间";三板小学"机电家族校园创客空间";小林实验小学"工艺与智造实验室"三灶中心小学"智能制造校园创客空间";海澄小学"航空体验馆")。其中,金湾一小的"多元跨学科综合校园创客空间"获得了珠海市"十佳青少年创客教育基地"称号。

"If the youth is strong, then the country will be strong; If the youth make progress, then the country will make progress". Today's world is based on science and technology. In order to train the future generation, Jinwan District pays attention to education of young children. From June 2016, five schools in Jinwan District, Jinwan NO. 1 Primary School, Sanban Primary School, Xiaolin Experimental Primary School, Sanzao Central Primary School and Haicheng Primary School, have established different themed maker labs. (Jinwan No. 1 Primary School's multi-disciplinary comprehensive campus creating maker space; Sanban Primary School's creating maker space of the mechanical and electrical family; Xiaolin Experimental Primary School's craftsmanship and intellectual building lab; Sanzao Central Primary School's intelligent campus creating maker space; and Haicheng Primary School's aeronautical experience exhibit). Among them, Jinwan No. 1 Primary School's "multi-disciplinary comprehensive campus creating maker space" won the title of "Top Ten Best Youth Maker Education Base" in Zhuhai City.

科技比赛现场
Science Competition Site

活动体验馆　Activity Experience Pavilion

　　亲爱的同学们,我们通过以上图文了解了金湾近些年的变化,你作为金湾的小主人,还能为大家说说你身边更多的变化吗? 你可以通过调查访问、观察、浏览互联网等方式,把你的新发现记录下来,跟大家一起分享。

　　My dear classes, we've got to know, through the above graphic, that Jinwan has changed in recent years. As the master of Jinwan, can you tell other people more changes around you? Through methods such as survey, observation, browsing the internet, please put down your new findings and share with everyone.

金湾的变化

The Great Changes in Jinwan

	以前 Before	现在 Now
饮食结构 Diet structure		
衣着打扮 Dressing up		
生活环境 Living environment		
日常活动 Daily activities		
交通工具 Transportation		
居住条件 Living condition		
教育水平 Education level		

附　　录

结　　题

　　本课题"走向世界——国际理解教育读本(初中版)实践研究"前后经过五年的时间,终于顺利结题。本课题立足于粤港澳大湾区经济一体化的历史背景下,旨在培养未来大湾区的建设者。今天的学生是明天的建设者,而基础教育更需要培养具有国际视野和"四个自信"(道路自信、理论自信、制度自信、文化自信)的建设者。

　　本课题具有如下特点。

　　一、以珠海市金湾区乡土资源和文化教育资源开发为载体,依据国家义务教育课程标准,以初中英语课堂教育教学为主渠道,以符合学生认知水平的中英文双语阅读为主要呈现方式,以爱国主义价值为基本教育取向,构建课堂内外相融合的创新形式,形成成果鲜明的教育教学特色。

　　二、在乡土教育资源开发过程中,坚持爱国主义导向,拓展学生思维空间和视野,形成国际理解意识与观念,为大湾区经济一体化建设奠定人才法制与道德根基。

　　三、体现以学生为主体的自我体验感悟的教育特色,重视自我探究的学习方式。学生层面示意图如附图 A-1 所示。

　　四、在推广实践中,成效显著。指导教师在探究中取长补短,挖掘外语教学学科领域的新问题,让师生在短时间内对世界各国的文化、历史、礼仪等有所了解,提升他们的国际化素养。

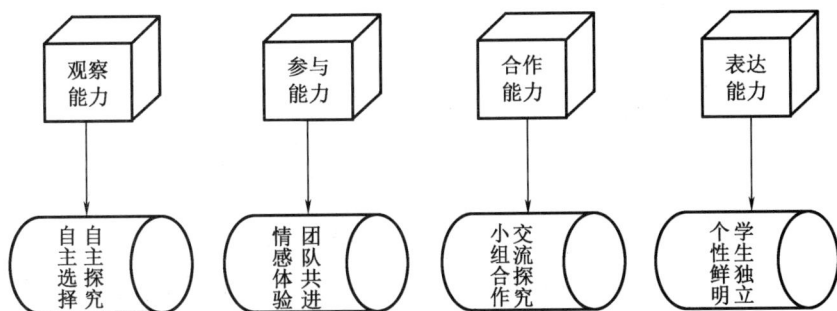

附图 A-1　学生层面示意图

五、适用对象及呈现形式(实践模型):"走向世界——国际理解教育读本(初中版)实践研究",融教学图文活动、情景生活、家庭、社会为一体,寓国际教育于乡土元素之中,每章四节,可以为教师教学开发教育资源,引导学生学习英语。在知识层面上,本课题既要对思想有全面的理解,又要上升到文化层面,而不只是事实和技能的获得。以形成性探究作为主要的学习方法,以跨学科主题作为知识框架,师生共同设计研究性的课程单元,学生经常在超越常规的学科范围内探求学科知识,使其形成重要的概念,获得技能和知识,培养正确的态度,学会对社会负责。

在教学中研究,在研究中教学,以德修身恪守师魂,以德修己弘扬师魂,以德育人桃李芬芳。经过多年的实践积累,使这个课题能够形成一部倡导传统文化、倡导国际教育理念,适合初中生阅读的双语国际理解教育的素材。这是金湾区本课程的一项重要成果,书中的每一个章节都是英语教师经过实践,并且在不断实践的过程中进一步改进和完善之后总结出来的。

首先,本书内容具有通俗性和趣味性,同时更具实用性。例如,在部分章节前面都有一定的知识简介、主题、特点、表现方法,以拓展学生的知识面。在语句结构上尽可能采用简洁的句式,并配以英文解说,尽可能减少技术性很强的乏味的语句,并配以图画,让学生一看就懂。

其次,充分体现了学生在学习过程中的主体性。不仅强调学生是教育和学习的主人,而且强调学生主动探索和创新的精神,让学生自我组织和互相启发,重视自主探究式学习方式。在展示评价中,我们设计了一些活动,学生在学的过程中得到肯定与鼓励,提升了他们的学习主动性。

课题研究流程图如附图 A-2 所示。

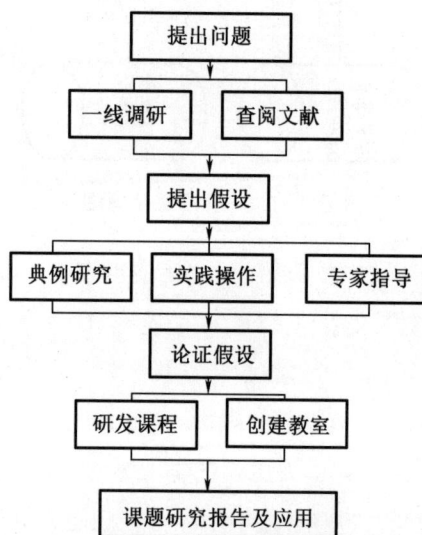

```
提出问题
  ↓
一线调研  查阅文献
  ↓
提出假设
  ↓
典例研究  实践操作  专家指导
  ↓
论证假设
  ↓
研发课程  创建教室
  ↓
课题研究报告及应用
```

附图 A-2　课题研究流程图

走向世界——区域国际理解教育课程构建研究报告

冯晓颖

【摘　　要】　金湾区为了让学生了解多元文化和全球问题等国际背景知识,在探究与体验的基础上,培养他们国际沟通与交往等方面的能力,培育他们的国际视野与中国意识,为其将来参与国际竞争与合作打下扎实的基础,进而提升全区各中小学教育国际化水平,扩大本区教育的国际影响,加速实现区域教育"国内一流、国际知名"的目标,需要构建区域的国际理解教育课程。

【关 键 词】　教育国际化;教育本土化;国际理解;文化素养

【作者简介】　冯晓颖,珠海市金湾区英语教研员、珠海市中学英语高级教师、教育部国培专家、珠海市名教师、珠海市先进教师、金湾区首批名教师、金湾区先进教师。研究领域为基础教育评价与评估,教育国际课程研究、基础教育英语研究。社会兼职有中国教育学会外语专业委员会指导委员、广东省教育学会外语专业委员会理事、广东省评价督导委员会理事、珠海市教育学会理事。发表著作、论文30多部(篇),累计300多万字。2010年7月主持立项的课题"基础教育英语教学评价试验项目研究",获教育部基础教育课程教材发展中心全国教学成果一等奖。

一、问题的提出

《国家中长期教育改革和发展规划纲要(2010—2020年)》指出要开展多层次、宽领域的教育交流与合作,提高我国教育国际化水平。金湾区作为珠海市的三个行政区之一,"建设幸福金湾"是其"十二五"期间发展的战略目标,"幸福教育"是其重要内容。而"幸福教育"的发展内涵之一是拥有较高水平的教育国际化,力求增强教育开放意识,建设教育国际化平台,加强国际交流与合作;开展国际理解教育,提高学校的教育国际化水平,在发展自身的基础上向世界展示金湾教育的成就。因此,构建区域性国际理解课程是新课程背景下金湾区教育发展的需要和必然。

二、研究目标、内容与方法

(一)研究目标

为了让学生了解多元文化和全球问题等国际背景知识,在探究与体验的基础上,培养他们国际沟通与交往等方面的能力,培育他们的国际视野与中国意识,为其将来参与国际竞争与合作打下扎实的基础,进而提升全区各中小学教育国际化水平,扩大本区教育的国际影响,构建区域的国际理解教育课程。

(二)国际理解教育课程的课程目标、课程内容、课程实施、课程评价等系列内容

1. 研究区域性国际理解教育课程的课程目标。该课程目标要适合于开放程度较高的珠海经济特区的特点。

2. 研究初中学生阶段国际理解教育的课程内容。该课程内容要综合考虑初中学生的价值观、知识领域等方面的布局与安排。

3. 研究进行的国际理解教育课程的实施。例如:如何安排课时、如何进行教学等。实施过程中,要突破重点、解决关键问题,构建金湾区第一套较为科学、完善,适用于初中生的国际理解教育用书。

(三)研究方法

1. 文献研究法:了解国际、国内理解教育研究的一般动向。

1945 年,联合国教科文组织成立,其章程规定:教育应在不同文化和种族之间促进人们的相互理解,依靠教育领域的国际合作促进和平。各国应采取行动,通过教育使其成员了解其他国家或民族的文化,把本国文化放在世界文化的背景下来理解,促进受教育者对于人类文化统一性的认识,意识到适用于各民族成员基本相同的生活条件和愿望,产生自己肩负的国际主义义务的责任感。

在此章程的指引下,1948 年 6 月,国际公共教育大会第 11 届会议在日内瓦召开。该会议建议各国教育部和其他教育当局应鼓励培养青少年的国际理解精神,并为有关以促进世界和平为己任的国际组织的教学提供帮助。

1974 年,第 18 届联合国教科文组织大会通过了《关于促进国际理解、合作

与和平的教育以及关于人权与基本自由的教育的建议》,倡导国际理解教育、和平与合作教育,在新的政治、经济和科技相互依赖的条件下深化和发展国际理解教育。

1981年,联合国教科文组织编写了《国际理解教育指南》,对国际理解教育的目标进行了明确界定,认为国际理解教育的主要目标是:"培养和平处事的人;培养具有人权意识的人;培养认识自己国家和具有国民自觉意识的人;理解其他国家、其他民族及其文化;认识国际相互依存关系与全国共同存在的问题,形成全世界的连带意识;养成具有国际协调、国际合作的态度并能实践。"

1994年,联合国教科文组织第44届国际教育大会在日内瓦召开。大会以"国际理解教育的总结与展望"为主题,以"为和平、人权和民主的教育"为中心内容,确立了新时期国际理解教育及相应的和平文化的内涵,并通过了《第44届国际教育大会宣言》《为和平、人权和民主的教育综合行动纲领》,为世界各国在新时期开展国际理解教育指明了方向。

到现在为止,许多国家都开设了国际理解教育课程。国际理解教育以培养跨文化交流的人才,以利于世界和平发展为目标,一方面重视知识、能力的传授;另一方面重视情感、态度、价值观的塑造。其主要特征有:国际理解教育是真正的文化对话;国际理解教育强调基本价值观的自我建构;国际理解教育强调动态的文化理解;国际理解教育倡导复归生活教育;国际理解教育倡导可持续发展的教育理念。

2. 调查研究法:调查教师和学生国际理解的知识的普及程度。

良好的师资是实施国际理解教育的关键所在,为此,英语教研员制定教师自主学习制度,加强教师对东西方文化的了解,培养英语教师在区域各项教育科研培训活动中实施国际理解教育的意识,提高英语教师的文化品位。学校聘请外教参与学校的英语教学,为青年教师创造浓郁的外语学习氛围。组织教师进行国际理解教育和双语教学的研讨,通过师生座谈、小组讨论、大会发言、邀请校外专家专题演讲等方式,介绍国内外国际理解教育的最新动态,借以领会和掌握其深刻含义。金湾区积极加强与发达国家和地区的教育教学的交流合作;与国际友好学校结成姐妹校,通过委派教师出国培训、参与或组建民间的教育网络、广泛开展国际交流与合作等方式,更好地提升学校教师与国际对话的能力。

3. 行动研究法：研究制定国际理解教育课程框架，编写国际理解教育用书并实施，然后反思、完善。

2012 年 9 月至 2013 年 6 月，初步挑选区域性国际理解教育研究团队，开展国际理解教育的文献研究，组织团队外出考察，通过"走出去、请进来"等多种形式解读国际理解教育，并制订课题申报实施计划。2013 年 6 月至 2014 年 7 月，编制国际理解教育课程框架，研究国际理解课程的内容、教学方式，编写、出版金湾区国际理解教育用书。2014 年 7 月至 2015 年 12 月，试用教学，研究课程实施的具体问题，撰写国际理解教育区域实施的研究报告。

三、成果的主要内容

（一）理论基础及主要观点

20 世纪初，德国社会学家韦伯曾经预言，随着人们追求效率的理性进程，科层制组织将会替代其他组织形态，成为主导型的组织形态，他用"铁笼"这个隐喻形象地描述了支配人们行为的某种不可抗拒的规则。到 20 世纪 80 年代初时，美国社会学家迪马吉奥和鲍威尔（DiMaggio and Powell）在《再访铁笼：组织领域的制度同构与集体理性》中重新回顾和对比了韦伯提出的"铁笼"原理，他们指出在后工业社会，由于国家和专业团体力量的增强，合法性逐渐取代了效率，成为起主导作用的组织生存和发展的新理性。本书利用组织分析中的有关理论，分析起源于西方国家的这个"铁笼"是如何被扩散到一个新的社会环境中创造和改变育人环境的能动性的。随着经济全球化进程的加快、信息技术的日新月异、世界一体化格局的逐步形成，教育国际化已经成为当今世界教育改革和发展的重要趋势。虽然对教育国际化的理论关注和实践探索最初更多地聚焦于高等教育，但是从 20 世纪 80 年代开始，基础教育国际化逐渐成为许多国家和地区基础教育改革的重点。

（二）实施策略

英语教师通过本书传递信息。从概念层面来看，我们让学生理解事物的形状、功能、事件的因果、物质的变化、人物与事件的联系，从国际视角承担国际公民的责任,反思自己的行为与礼仪;培养学生思考、交流、社交、调研、自我管理的技能,让学生感受、珍惜自己的真实情感,表现出宽容、尊重、正直、独立、热情、共鸣、好奇、创造、合作、自信、投入、感激的态度。从知识层面来看,既要对思想进行全面理解,又要上升到文化层面,不能只追求技能和结果的获得。在学习过程中,以形成性探究作为主要的学习方法,以跨学科主题作为知识框架,师生共同设计研究性的单元课题,学生能够实现跨学科探求知识的目的。通过以上学习过程,学生能够在获得知识和技能的同时,培养正确的学习态度,学会对社会负责。

(三) 适用对象与呈现形式(实践模型)

本书符合英语课程内容六要素。主题是学习语言最重要的内容,英语教学活动就是对有关中外文化的意义进行探究、编写体例、寻找主题。主题为人与自我、人与社会、人与自然。在人与自我方面,从教会学生生活,指导学生学习、做人、做事等入手。在人与社会方面,关注社会服务、人际沟通、文学、艺术、历史、文化、科学、技术等。在人与自然方面,重视自然生态、环境保护、灾害防范、宇宙探索。在反复实践中,初中英语教师更加关注的是语言技能、语言知识、文化意识、情感态度、学习策略等内容。2017 年 7 月,《普通高中课程方案及课程标准》(简称《课程标准》)颁布后,课题实验教师调整思路,使课题内容更加清晰。《课程标准》中提到了英语学科核心素养四要素的关系:语言能力是基础要素,从听说读写看、理解和表达、语言意识、语感四方面培养能力。文化意识反映了价值取向,从中外文化理解和优秀文化认同中体现。思维品质见心智特征,包括逻辑性思维、批判性思维、创新性思维。学习能力是发展条件,包括调适学习策略、拓宽学习渠道、提升学习效率等内容。

(四)重大进展和突破

1. 理念层面

有大学科观的理念,有特色鲜明的教程,有完善和正在完善的学科构建细节。研磨英语课程内容的六大要素,分别为:主题语境(人与自我、人与自然、人与社会)、语篇类型(内容素材、多种文体、多模态)、语言知识(语音词汇、语法、语篇语用)、文化知识(物质文化、精神文化、多种中外文化)、语言技能(听、说、读、写、看)、学习策略(元认知、交际、情感策略)。

2.教师层面

一是了解英语教师在教育国际化过程中的思想、行为、价值观等方面的情况,全程参与本书编写与课程实施;二是建设具有国际化元素的区域文化,设计润物无声的双语环境文化。把区域打造成中西文化荟萃的、具有"国际味"的大观园,并从中认识世界,学会交流,拓宽国际视野;三是促进教师专业化发展,利用国际理解教育的多渠道,借助英语学科教学中的通融性、学科知识的同一性的特点,组织同伴互助、资源分享,在探究中取长补短、互通有无,共同提高研究能力,发掘学科领域的新问题,共同提高国际交往的能力。

3.呈现层面

在教育国际化进程中,开发如世界各国礼仪、文化习俗等区本双语课程,让学生在短时间内对世界各国的文化、历史、礼仪等有所了解,进而提升学生的国际化素养。

四、研究反思

1. 对教育国际化认识不够,需要增加国际教育理念培训

受传统教育观念的影响,很多人认为学校要以传统学科课程(语、数、外等)为主,特别是国际理解教育课程刚刚启动之时,老师们的精力主要集中在传统学科课程的设置与实验上。

2. 英语教师队伍建设问题

双语对老师的外语能力提出了挑战,这需要我们英语教师加强英语口语运用能力,以及对学生学习英语能力的考察和培养。

五、结语

本课题的开发与研究是一项长期的工作,在这个过程中,我们克服了各方面的困难,也激发了对课程改革的更多思考。学生们喜爱这门课程,尤其是潜能生在这门课程中表现出前所未有的热情,他们善于创作、乐于表达,在活动过程中不断成长。"发展"是面向所有学生的"发展",在课程改革火热开展的今天,在强调教育技术的今天,我们确实应该更科学、更理性地开展我们的教育工作,以"学生为本",寻求最能激发学生学习兴趣的教育形式,做好我们的国际理解教育课程的构建与研发。

参 考 文 献

[1] 蔡明德,刘振天,刘玉彬,等.语码转换:双语教学新模式[J].教育研究,
2007,28(9):90-94.

[2] 叶澜."新基础教育"探索性研究报告集[M].上海:三联书店,1999.

[3] 教育部基础教育司,教育部师范教育司.新课程的理念与创新[M].北京:
高等教育出版社,2004.

[4] DIMAGGIO P J, POWELL W W. The iron cage revisited:institutional
isomorphism and collective rationality in organizational fields[J]. American
sociological review, 1983,48(2): 147-160.

[5] 马克斯·韦伯.新教伦理与资本主义精神[M].于晓,陈维纲,译.北京:
生活·读书·新知三联书店, 1987.

后 记

　　长期以来,珠海市金湾区英语教师大力开展课题研究,为本书的出版做了大量的工作,在此谨向付出努力的各位同人和前辈深表感谢和敬意。

　　此课题是广东省中小学新一轮"百千万人才培养工程"项目的专项课题。本课题的顺利完成,离不开理论导师华南师范大学黄丽燕教授、广东第二师范学院李华教授、吴慧坚教授,实践导师冯页、孙新的指导。衷心感谢教授和导师一直以来不遗余力地对我们初中英语教研员的帮助和提携!

　　感谢承担调查问卷编制、资料收集、归类整理工作的东北大学理学院学生李東璨同学,以及负责文字校对审核的珠海市教育研究院的英语教研员李昂老师。参与课题研究与实践的一线教师有:王玉琳、王艳伶、叶爱琴、刘罗斯、孙佳丽、李广玉、李顺姬、李悦媚、肖佳妮、吴春梅、吴新梅、何瑞妮、张玉芬、林江凌、胡芳、洪宇、郭淑娴、曾程程、曾瑾、温海苑、邓媛媛等。

　　由于作者水平有限,书中难免有不成熟甚至错误的地方,敬请读者指正!

冯晓颖

2020 年 9 月 4 日于珠海